CHRIST'S SECOND COMING

Christ's Second Coming

SEVEN CRUCIAL QUESTIONS

WHO?

WHAT?

WHY?

HOW?

WHEN?

WHERE?

HOW CAN WE BE PREPARED?

Donald CB Cameron, BTh MA PhD

40 Beansburn, Kilmarnock, Scotland

ISBN-13: 978 1 910513 92 7

Copyright © 2017 by John Ritchie Ltd.
40 Beansburn, Kilmarnock, Scotland

www.ritchiechristianmedia.co.uk

Scripture quotations marked "NKJV" are taken from the New King James Version®. Copyright© by Thomas Nelson, Inc. Used by permission. All rights reserved.

All rights reserved. No part of this publication may be reproduced, stored in a retrievable system, or transmitted in any form or by any other means – electronic, mechanical, photocopy, recording or otherwise – without prior permission of the copyright owner.

Typeset by John Ritchie Ltd., Kilmarnock
Printed by Bell & Bain Ltd., Glasgow

Dedicated to friends and family who may or may not yet have trusted in the Lord Jesus Christ as their Saviour.

Contents

Foreword	9
The Books of the Bible	11
PART ONE – THE FACTS OF THE SECOND COMING	15
1. God's Right to Intervene Before Catastrophe	15
2. A Second Coming?	17
3. Seven Urgent Questions and Answers	20
a. Who?	20
b. What?	21
c. How?	21
d. Why?	21
e. When?	22
f. Where?	22
4. The Writing on the Wall	23
a. Harbingers of Environmental Judgments	26
b. Global Depravity	27
c. Degeneracy Within 'Christendom' or Formerly Christian Nations	29
d. Luke-Warmness Within Churches	31
e. Israel in the Eye of the Storm	33
PART TWO – BIBLICAL EVIDENCE AND BRIEF OVERVIEW OF THE END TIMES	35
5. The Miracle of Predictive Prophecy	35
6. Old Testament End-Time Prophecies	39

Christ's Second Coming

7. New Testament End-Time Prophecies	41
8. The Duration of Christ's First and Second Comings	45
9. The Sequence of Events at Christ's Second Coming	48
10. The Opening Event of Christ's Second Coming	49
11. The Climactic Event of Christ's Second Coming	54
12. Between the Opening and Climactic Events – In Heaven	58
13. Between the Opening and Climactic Events – On Earth	61
14. Satan's Final Bid for Godhood	65
15. Israel – The Side-Lined Chosen People	68
16. Whoso Readeth, Let Him Understand	72
17. Israel's Final Holocaust and Restoration	77
18. The Year of the Lord's Redeemed	81
19. The Holy City, the New Jerusalem	85
PART THREE – ARE WE READY FOR CHRIST'S RETURN?	88
20. The Authority for our Confidence	88
21. Our Personal Options	91
BRIEF CHRONOLOGY OF MAIN EVENTS COVERED IN THIS BOOK	94

Foreword

As someone who came to faith in Christ fifty years ago through the message of the Second Coming I am more than pleased to endorse this latest work from the pen of Donald C.B. Cameron whom I know as an enthusiast and something of an 'expert' on these issues.

This book has been written with the design that it should point people to the Saviour and to make them aware of the fact that time may be short. The message of Christ's return brings a sense of urgency to the gospel and Donald communicates this fact in these pages.

I found part one very interesting in that it covers the same facts that I used in a recent sermon entitled, 'The mechanics of the Lord's return' i.e the what, why, where, how and when of His coming. These points give a simple appraisal of the subject for those who may have little understanding of these things.

Donald's comprehensive list of signs of the times should in itself be a revelation to the unbeliever and give the reader real food for thought. The many things that he has listed cannot be easily ignored and are clear pointers to this coming great event.

In part two he takes us into the sequence of God's prophetic programme and accurately and faithfully outlines coming events in accord with our pre-millennial and pre-tribulational understanding of prophecy. In this section he also focuses on Israel which has often been referred to as 'God's Timepiece' and which is key to the understanding of dispensational truth to which the writer adheres.

Such a book would be incomplete without some sort of appeal and Donald's invitation to the reader, to put his/her faith in Jesus Christ as Saviour forms a fitting conclusion to the work. I believe the book fills a gap in the market in its appeal to believers with little understanding of the subject and in its attempt to reach the unbeliever as well. Donald has fulfilled both objectives admirably and it is my prayer that many will be brought into the fellowship of the saints through this book.

Rev Colin Le Noury
General Director/Prophetic Witness Movement International.

THE BOOKS OF THE BIBLE

THE OLD TESTAMENT

Genesis	Gen
Exodus	Ex
Leviticus	Lev
Numbers	Num
Deuteronomy	Deut
Joshua	Josh
Judges	Judg
Ruth	Ruth
1st Samuel	I Sam
2nd Samuel	II Sam
1st Kings	I Kings
2nd Kings	II Kings
1st Chronicles	I Chron
2nd Chronicles	II Chron
Ezra	Ezra
Nehemiah	Neh
Esther	Esth
Job	Job
Psalms	Ps
Proverbs	Prov
Ecclesiastes	Eccles
Song of Solomon	S of S
Isaiah	Isa
Jeremiah	Jer
Lamentations	Lam
Ezekiel	Ezek
Daniel	Dan
Hosea	Hos

Christ's Second Coming

Joel	Joel
Amos	Amos
Obadiah	Obad
Jonah	Jonah
Micah	Mic
Nahum	Nah
Habakkuk	Hab
Zephaniah	Zeph
Haggai	Hag
Zechariah	Zech
Malachi	Mal

THE NEW TESTAMENT

Matthew	Matt
Mark	Mk
Luke	Lk
John	Jn
Acts	Acts
Romans	Rom
1st Corinthians	I Cor
2nd Corinthians	II Cor
Galatians	Gal
Ephesians	Eph
Philippians	Phil
Colossians	Col
1st Thessalonians	I Thess
2nd Thessalonians	II Thess
1st Timothy	I Tim
2nd Timothy	II Tim
Titus	Titus
Hebrews	Hebrews
James	Jas
1st Timothy	I Tim

2nd Timothy	II Tim
Titus	Titus
Philemon	Philem
Hebrews	Heb
James	Jas
1st Peter	I Pet
2nd Peter	II Pet
1st John	I Jn
2nd John	II Jn
3rd John	III Jn
Jude	Jude
Revelation	Rev

Christ's Second Coming

PART ONE

THE FACTS OF THE SECOND COMING

1. GOD'S RIGHT TO INTERVENE BEFORE DISASTER

Millions believe that Jesus Christ is coming back, and that one day every knee will have to bow before Him and confess that He is Lord. If you think that this is unlikely or impossible, please read on.

The question, "Do you want the good news or the bad news first?" may introduce a joke or be the opening gambit of a serious conversation. This is anything but a joking matter; it is desperately serious. The bad news is that the world is due to get worse, much worse to the point of near extinction, before it gets better. There are in contrast three major items of good news: (1) While God hates sin, He still loves sinners; (2) He has provided a way of escape before the worst happens; (3) Beyond the coming crisis there is to be a golden age of peace before the end of the world. But in the nearer future only the personal intervention of the Lord Jesus Christ is going to prevent life on earth from self-destruction. He Himself has stated that this will be so.

People called atheists do not believe in God. That is their problem inasmuch as their lack of belief has no impact whatsoever on God's existence; and one day they, like everyone else, will have to meet Him. People called deists believe in God, but assume that He is largely indifferent to humanity and leaves us entirely to our own devices, rather than intervening in history. People called theists believe not only that He exists, but that He is intensely interested in humanity and, in His own times and ways, frequently intervenes, even although this may not be recognised. Sometimes He has done so dramatically and decisively in history. Often He intervenes in mercy and often in judgment, and sometimes in both at the same time, when both oppressor and oppressed are involved, thus bringing both relief and despair.

There are numerous indications that He will intervene thus in the very near future. These we will explore at Section 4. However we must emphasise that we are given no data to say precisely when this will happen, except that it will be before earth's darkest hour, rather than its brightest. Forget about secret codes and occult messages; the main facts are plain to see if we want to.

The calendar almost universally accepted in this world tacitly recognises that history is divided Into what happened before and what happened after the birth of Jesus Christ. In 2002 the secular world, in order to avoid acknowledging this fact, adopted the new title CE, meaning either Common Era or Current Era. Such denial is foolish, futile and dangerous.

Two thousand years ago God came unassumingly and unpretentiously in the person of the Lord Jesus Christ. When Christ comes again, majestically and in judgment, none will be able to hide from His presence or fail to acknowledge His authority. None can opt out.

This is my eleventh and shortest book. It is written specifically for young Christians, non-Christians, and those on the fringe of Christianity, but others may find it helpful. Please understand that, especially in the first part, I am catering for readers with very little knowledge of the Bible; so I ask those who are more familiar with the Scriptures to appreciate that I am not trying to patronise. Writing for unbelievers at least as much as for believers is not an easy balance to maintain!

I realise that some readers will find it old fashioned, but, unless otherwise indicated, I shall use mainly the 1611 Authorised (King

James) Version of the Bible, as there are no copyright problems, and I believe that the words of Holy Scripture can communicate much more eloquently and infinitely more authoritatively than those of any individual theologian. Occasionally, where the AV/KJV rendering is inaccurate or so dated as to be unhelpful, I will use the New King James Version (NKJV) and indicate this in brackets.

Please note that I am adhering to mainstream Christian teaching, albeit a neglected part of that teaching. Several New Testament passages foretell a generally declining or lukewarm Church at the end of the age, but Jesus never advocated planting a brand new church, which is what the cults have tried to do. Repentance and reformation are often appropriate; reinvention is not. Therefore I am not promoting the fanciful inventions of some of the 19th Century mainly American cults, such as Mormons, Seventh Day Adventists and 'Jehovah's Witnesses', with their parodies of Christianity, private agendas and faulty and illicit formulae for calculating dates. All have been discredited.

When throughout this book I refer to 'Church' with a capital 'C', I mean *"The Church of God, which he hath purchased with his own blood"* (Acts 20:28) – in other words exclusively believers. A small 'c is used when writing of denominations, which can be made up of both believers and unbelievers.

2. A SECOND COMING?

The Bible contains the only reliable information about the future. God has generously provided sufficient for our needs, but not enough to satisfy our curiosity. It tells of God's mercy and His judgment, about His love and the option of accepting or turning away from that love. It tells us about the alternatives of rescue and disaster, and of a world with life on the brink of extinction and the just-in-time Divine intervention which will provide, for those who survive the crisis, global restoration beyond our wildest dreams.

Christ's Second Coming

Here is something intensely relevant to everyone, whether young or old, saint or sinner, eager or indifferent, Christian or non-Christian, even dead or alive! It is becoming a matter of extreme urgency. Yet, although it is to be the most spectacular, awe-inspiring, world-shattering event or series of events, many of those entrusted with proclaiming its potential imminence and implications remain silent, or pay the minimum lip service. However, as we shall see, that is precisely what the Bible leads us to expect for what it calls the latter days.

God has declared certain facts, as is His right as Creator. People may close their eyes to great truths, but that will not be accepted as an excuse when the time comes. The sinister pressures upon Christians to minimise the study and proclamation of these matters goes back many centuries and largely escaped the attention of the great Reformers, or at least their immediate successors. Indeed, some of those who would now class themselves as reformed are among the main offenders. While it is infinitely more important that we should be ready than that we should be experts on the Second Coming, we must not share Jesus' condemnation of the religious leaders of His day, who could forecast the weather accurately, but were indifferent to the signs given in their Scriptures regarding His First Coming. Paul could declare: *"I have not shunned to declare unto you all the counsel of God"* (Acts 20:27). We know from his epistles that this is true. Churches which fail to declare Second Coming truth proportionate to the space devoted to it in Scripture take on a huge responsibility.

The term Second Coming does not actually occur in the Bible, although words like come/coming and return/returning are frequently found. Jesus said: *"If I go..... I will come again"* (Jn 14:3 – a verse which we shall quote in full later. Second Advent means the same thing, of course, using the Latin derived word for coming. An awareness of the happenings of Christ's First Coming should influence our expectations of the Second, even if we perceive huge contrasts between the two. Most people

Part One - The Facts Of The Second Coming

in what were once considered Christian countries know that Jesus lived on earth around two thousand years ago. To say that He "came" at that time implies that He had previously been somewhere else and that He came from there to here. Sadly "Father Christmas", mistletoe and other pagan winter festival trivia obscure the basic First Coming facts for some people. In many other respects His First Coming provides a splendid precedent for His Second. Although they are not necessary, I am using capital letters in this book for First and Second Coming and certain related themes for emphasis.

At the outset I have to remind myself that, no matter how skilful I may be as a writer, no matter how clever a debater or how expert an apologist, if readers do not want to believe in Christ's Second Coming, they simply will not. Even the Apostle Paul, who really was the most convincing of Christian advocates, had to concede that *"The world by wisdom knew not God."* Peter, in his Second Epistle, chapter 3, speaks of scoffing and wilful or deliberate ignorance regarding these matters. But others can be thrilled when they begin to comprehend what God has in store, and come to appreciate how merciful God is already being in preserving our race from destruction.

I have divided this book into numbered sections for speedy cross-reference. I have covered most of the subject matter in greater detail and in specialised ways in other books. But here I want to concentrate on the fundamentals, allowing the words of Holy Scripture to answer many of the questions with fewer and shorter comments from me. I also want to point out why, more than ever before, we should be on our toes either in eager anticipation or in trepidation. I will cover the entire end-time programme, but will concentrate on the great opening and culminating events of the Second Coming and summarise the intervening ones more briefly. Two sections will be dedicated to what is to happen after the Second Coming. Most importantly, in the final two sections I wish to summarise the basis of Christian faith, the grounds for our confidence, and finally to remind readers of how they can be fully prepared right here and now. Jesus told his disciples: *"When ye shall hear of wars and commotions, be not terrified: for these things must first come to pass"* (Lk 21:9); but then He went on to talk of *"Men's hearts failing them for fear, and for looking after those things which are coming on the earth"* (v 26). As we shall be reminded, this is more than just the believers' confidence in God; they have a prior prophecy to which to look forward with joy.

Ultimately every single person on earth will be affected by both Christ's past First and future Second Comings. That is because He is not only the Son of God; He is also God the Son; He is omnipotent, and what He has promised He will do! Following centuries of restraint, His Second Coming, like His First, will take place *"in the fullness of time"* or at the appropriate moment.

3. SEVEN URGENT QUESTIONS AND ANSWERS

Let us consider some of the basic facts of Christ's Second Coming. I am deliberately keeping the answers brief and succinct at this juncture; they can all be expanded and the evidence presented beginning at Section 5. But here I am using Kipling's trusted simple formula of What? Why? When? How? Where? and Who? though not in that sequence. I shall leave to the end of the book a seventh exceptionally important question – what can we be doing about it in the meantime?

3.a. WHO?

The One who has promised to return personally is the Lord Jesus Christ, the eternal, Divine Son of God, who two thousand years ago temporarily veiled His glory in order to become like one of us, lived a sinless life, was rejected, betrayed, crucified and died, before rising again and returning to the sphere from whence He had come. He is coming again chiefly in His capacity as the Son of Man who is King of Kings and Lord of Lords. He is the Saviour of the world, especially of those who believe on Him. Everyone without exception will be deeply affected;

each one of us is answerable to our Creator. Every individual must appear before Him, though not all in the same way or at the same time.

3.b. WHAT?

Christ's future return is to be the most dramatic Divine intervention in human history. It is in fact God's alternative to the global extinction which humankind is effectively bringing upon itself with increasing rapidity. The potential repercussions of human actions are incalculable. As at His First Coming, His Second Coming will involve a number of years. It involves both a 'coming for' and a 'coming to'. Just as His First Coming reached a climax, with His death and resurrection, so His Second Coming will reach a climax, with His visible, bodily descent to the earth. But again, just like His First Coming, much of immense importance is to happen before the climax. It will constitute the fulfilment of a host of both Old and New Testament prophecies covering many contrasting happenings.

3.c. HOW?

In contrast to His humble birth in a stable, His lowly lifestyle and a shameful sin-bearing death on a cross at His First Coming, so His Second Coming will be glorious, triumphant and universally visible, bringing either joy or terror, salvation or destruction to those upon earth, depending upon where they stand individually in relation to Him. He is coming followed by the awesome armies of Heaven. As to how it will be accomplished, we need not enquire, as the coming One has all the resources, visible and invisible, of Heaven and earth at His command.

3.d. WHY?

He is returning to bring the present age to a close, when the earth is ready for harvesting, and when the "wheat" or weeds, which have been growing together throughout the long Church Age are "ripe". He is coming to raise believers from the dead in the First Resurrection, He is coming to put down rebellion, to rule with a rod of iron and to imprison the Devil, Satan. He is coming to establish universal peace. He is coming to restore a devastated earth and to usher in a golden age. He is coming to establish "on earth as it is in Heaven" the Kingdom which has been hitherto "in mystery", and so much more.

3.e. WHEN?

The short answer is that nobody upon earth knows the time of the great opening event of the Second Coming. Christ made that very clear indeed, and the various attempts to calculate the timing is sheer defiance, and has led to the birth of two major cults. The timing of the climactic event will also be unknown as to the day and hour, but there will be very specific indicators as to when it is imminent. However, even now we are given certain "signs of the times" to keep us on our toes. Never have these signs, we believe, been so vivid and portentous, with widespread terror of global disaster, and total annihilation now believed possible even within secular society.

3.f. WHERE?

Since His ascension, Christ has been in His Father's House (Heaven), where He has been preparing a place to which He will take collectively His own resurrected and surviving living redeemed. Heaven is part of a different creation, invisible to us, where distances as we understand them are irrelevant and where the interface with our creation is controlled by God. The souls, but not yet the bodies, of believers have been in a resting place in Heaven since death. He is to re-enter this creation both at a meeting in the clouds of the air, and later to the surface of the planet itself. The epicentre of the battle which will be raging when He returns to earth will be at

Armageddon in Northern Israel; but His feet will alight on the Mount of Olives on the outskirts of Jerusalem.

4. THE WRITING ON THE WALL

The potent Babylonian tyrant, Nebuchadnezzar, was privileged to have revealed, through a dream interpreted by Daniel, God's plans for a succession of empires which would hold sway over Israel (Daniel 2). Later he had to be reminded forcibly that *"the most High ruleth in the kingdom of men, and giveth it to whomsoever he will"* (4:32). His grandson, Belshazzar, was fully aware of the details and, as Daniel later pointed out, without excuse. Yet this profane king deliberately chose the golden vessels plundered from the Jerusalem Temple for a blasphemous drunken orgy with a thousand of his nobles: *"In the same hour came forth fingers of a man's hand.....and the king saw the part of the hand that wrote. Then the king's countenance was changed, and his thoughts troubled him, so that the joints of his loins were loosed, and his knees smote one against another"* (5:5-6). The aged prophet was called to interpret: *"God hath numbered thy kingdom, and finished it....."* (5:26). Belshazzar was slain that very night.

Sooner or later God intervenes decisively against defiance, particularly when it comes from those who have reason to know better. Within Christendom parliaments, judiciaries and now leaders within major churches are taking it upon themselves, not simply to break God's laws, something which has always happened, but to defy them openly, flaunting and promoting the resultant sin. Surely the writing is on the wall. Many millions still stand for the truth, but in some denominations this amounts to a rearguard action. There are church leaders whose bowels should be melting and their knees knocking.

Jesus Christ will come at a point when the world in general will least expect Him. But believers are told to look forward to His coming and ever to be ready. We must keep an eye on world events which should heighten our expectations. Jesus told us to look up when we begin to see certain dramatic events come to pass, rather than to wait until disaster is imminent. In other words we should be looking forward to the first of the great events which are to occur at His coming, rather than the final ones.

Before proceeding further, I wish to make an important point, to avoiding misunderstandings. Despite the many signs of the times or portents which we are about to consider, we must recognise that the world has not yet plummeted to its lowest moral level; that is to happen only after the opening event of Christ's Second Coming. There is still much good in the world and resistance to the worst brands of evil. The public reaction to such atrocities as the May 2017 Manchester suicide bombing, and the willing help given, bear testimony to this. After the opening event of the Second Coming, which could occur at any time, there will be an ever increasingly sharp divide between the moral and spiritual condition of those who have newly become believers and those who remain unbelievers, with stark choices to be made between God and Satan, between Christ and Antichrist. Then there will be no middle ground, no nominal believers.

There is still widespread resistance within Christendom to the signs of the times. Back in 1867 that great theologian, Bishop JC Ryle, wrote: "I fully admit that the gospel appears to make rapid progress in some countries; but that it ever does more than call out an elect people, I utterly deny. It never did more in the days of the Apostles." The world is to be evangelised, but certainly not converted, before the climactic event of Christ's Second Coming. Each year thousands of churches celebrate what they call Holy Week, from Palm Sunday to Easter, remembering the incredibly important events of Jesus' crucifixion and resurrection, but completely ignoring much the longest discourse which Jesus gave during the original Holy Week, the Olivet Discourse, which in some detail foretells His Second Coming.

When I was fourteen years of age, the sun and moon turned bright blue for several hours in northern England and southern

Part One - The Facts Of The Second Coming

Scotland; huge forest fires in Canada were thought to be the cause. When I saw the blue sun, I sprinted to the farmhouse to tell my mother that the Lord Jesus was about to return. I had been vaguely aware of Joel's prophecy: *"The sun shall be turned into darkness, and the moon into blood, before the great and the terrible day of the LORD come"* (2:31). My faith on that occasion was not at fault, but I had got my colours wrong! Though not a great student of Bible prophecy, my mother always looked forward to the Lord's return, and was sufficiently committed to the signs of the times to turn to her Bible to find out for herself and for me. We were both disappointed, but reassured that the prophecy had not failed!

Now readers may reasonably ask why we should be more expectant now than in recent centuries or decades. Of course many of the following things have occurred before, and the latter day scoffers whom Peter predicted will always find excuses for turning a blind eye. But what is significant, since I first heard of the signs of the times back in the 'forties, is the number of them occurring together, and the sheer intensity and speed of acceleration of some of them. Much of what science is trying to remedy was in the first place the result of sin, and, without recognition of this and repentance, there can be no lasting reversal by human efforts of what is in effect judgment.

Recently I reviewed what I had written in 2007, in my longer book, *"The Day of Vengeance of our God and Earth's Golden Age Beyond",* when the scripturally unjustified euphoria of the "new millennium" was subsiding. It strikes me forcibly that in the intervening ten years none of the features included has become less noticeable, and that several have actually intensified, whilst dramatic unexpected new ones have appeared. Even over the few months of writing this book in early 2017 the pace seems to have further quickened. I reprint and expand that list below with up-dating comments for each section. Inevitably there will be some duplication as a number of signs fit into more than one category. Many are very complex issues, and I have had to present them very briefly. The list is not exhaustive; readers may think of others.

4.a. HARBINGERS OF ENVIRONMENTAL JUDGMENTS:

- Global warming leading both to droughts and increased moisture retention.
- Freak weather conditions and breaking of previous records becoming accepted as normal.
- Increased hurricanes, tsunamis, floods.
- Seismic activity – earthquakes and continental plate pressures with colossal potential for damage to modern infrastructures.
- Growing desert and arid regions engulfing whole nations.
- Shrinking ice-caps with potential for massive flooding elsewhere.
- The global environment being systematically destroyed.
- Denuding of mineral and other natural resources at an utterly unsustainable level.
- Increasingly unpredictable growing and harvesting conditions.
- Many areas of severe famine and malnutrition despite scientific advances.
- Increasingly depleted fish stocks in ever more lethally polluted seas and rivers.
- Serious lack of drinking water in several regions with little prospect of adequate remedies.
- Colossal extravagant wastage and dumping of food while millions are starving.
- Fear of asteroid strikes, giant meteorite and possibly comet strikes.
- New resistant diseases appearing as quickly as old ones are eliminated.

2017 Up-Date:
- Greater areas of Africa unable to feed themselves through drought and failed harvests.

Part One - The Facts Of The Second Coming

- Unprecedented level of flooding in parts of the Indian sub-continent resulting in crop failures.
- Ever diminishing numbers of bees, butterflies and other insects essential for pollination.
- Food supply systems in richer countries very vulnerable thanks to ever increasing dependence on wasteful air-freighting of seasonal foods from other lands.
- Surrender of technological initiative and production skills to China in many key areas, for greed and profit, irrespective of long term cost and consequences.
- Widespread recognition among politicians, economists, agriculturalists, meteorologists, conservationists, environmentalists, armament specialists of all the above, but no recognition by them of almighty God who has all things under His control.

4.b. **GLOBAL DEPRAVITY**
- Open defiance against the Creator.
- Human ability to destroy all life on planet.
- Despite UN Security Council, NATO etc, numerous local wars.
- The existence of rogue nations like North Korea, having weapons of mass destruction and delivery means.
- God dishonouring religions fired by and inciting hatred, and rejoicing in inflicting pain, death, chaos and destruction in the name of their particular deity.
- In Arab Spring lands greatly increased persecution of Christian minorities with the ultimate goal of their elimination.
- Child soldiers and terrorists – incitement to hatred from the cradle.
- Inter-racial tensions, strife and hatred.
- People trafficking, mainly for prostitution, largely of women and children, or the human organ trade.
- Convenience abortions, especially of unwanted females, accepted as normal, some countries having more abortions than live births.

- Slave trade, forced labour, child labour, debt bondage.
- Hindu caste system – 250,000,000 "untouchables".
- Biometrics – human manipulation of DNA and other building blocks of creation.
- Technocrats developing artificial intelligence without fully understanding the implications.

2017 Up-Date:
- Recovery from the 2008 banking and economic depression, much of it fuelled by human greed, has been only partial, with no prospect of recovery on the horizon. Nations simply cannot afford to fund essential responsibilities.
- Virtual end of détente between Capitalist and Communist Blocs, especially NATO and Russia, the latter with renewed imperial ambitions leading to creeping aggression in Ukraine and controlling of Caucasus routes to the Middle East, after a brief acquaintance with democracy.
- Failure of the initially applauded 2010 "Arab Spring" to bring peace, prosperity and stability to certain Muslim lands, with escalation of Sunni-Shi'ite conflict, complicated by national ambitions and rivalries.
- Atrocities perpetrated to prove that the Muslim god, Allah, is "great" by the very people, in particular the Saudi bankrolled ultra-fundamentalist Wahhabist Salafi-Jihadists, who go out of the way to make his name repugnant to the world, thus themselves "insulting" him.
- Resulting waves of both genuine refugees and economic migrants, swamping some of the recipient nations and providing cover for merciless, undiscriminating terrorism.
- Global indifference to the plight of persecuted Christians in Muslim lands. Failure within formerly Christian lands to give such refugees, who pose no terrorist threat, preferential status and protection reflects the moral bankruptcy and cowardice of Christendom.
- The terrifying prospect of ISIS launched drone weapons.

- Entire global infrastructure vulnerable to incapacitating, malevolent cyberattacks. The acceleration of this menace over the past ten years and potential for future development should make the unbeliever tremble.
- God, who long ago confused human language, when the builders of Babel defied His command to multiply and fill the earth, could, should He so wish, similarly confuse modern communications and contribute to global disasters such as the Revelation chapter 18 destruction of Babylon the Great.
- Closely related, the ability of unseen powers to exert influence over individuals through nano-technology is quite unprecedented and points, among other things, to the prophesied Mark of the Beast of Revelation 13.
- Most nations and individuals wanting to spend more than they earn, with consequent mounting debt. Trivial luxuries are assumed to be necessities and "poverty" often, but not always, has ceased to mean deprival of staple requirements.
- Human rights vigorously defended in law, even when criminals have offended the rights of others and ignored their human responsibilities.
- Claims of imminent ability to produce genetically modified "designer babies".
- As my friend Dr Bill Freel says, "We live in a society that has gone sour and a civilisation that has gone sick. The scent of death is upon our planet and our own nation is imperiled from within and without. Many people have responded to the agonized conclusion that the individual does not matter, and, if there is a God, He does not care about them."

4.c. DEGENERACY WITHIN CHRISTENDOM OR FORMERLY CHRISTIAN NATIONS:

- Equal status for all religions - multi-faith approach, even sometimes in Christian schools.
- Failure to distinguish between God, who *"spared not his own Son, but delivered him up for us all"* and Allah,

- who is emphasised as "having no son" and is seen to be honoured by Jihadism.
- Rejection of the Sabbath or Sunday as a day set apart.
- Increasing legislation against active personal evangelisation.
- Flaunting perversions which the Bible declares to be abominations.
- Overturning of Ten Commandments at European parliamentary level.
- The 'right' to practise what God states to be sin enshrined in law.
- Failure to balance human rights with human responsibilities.
- The right of the criminal greater than that of the victim.
- The God-given responsibility of the loving parent to chastise the child as necessary forbidden by recent laws.
- Denial of the status of human embryos, which have bodies, souls and spirits.
- Departure from marriage as the norm, 'partner' status, one parent 'families'.
- Euthanasia by personal choice, far beyond the mere closure of life support systems.
- Persistence in teaching evolution despite massive contrary evidence.
- Growth of Eastern mysticism, yoga, transcendental meditation and New Age practices.
- Horoscopes, tarot cards and allied occult devices more respected than the Bible.
- Escalation of Satanism in Europe, often initially through a mixture of black magic, hard drugs, sex and sometimes "heavy metal".

2017 Up-Date:
- There is growing hatred, bitterness and nihilism even within what have long been considered democracies. Democracy is being used as a shield for personal autocratic ambition and self-aggrandisement.

- Nationalism, separatism and xenophobia are being pursued by exploiting grievances, actual and imaginary, as with Nazism eighty years ago, rather than by spontaneous positive patriotism.
- Sportspeople and entertainers with no supplementary talents are paid immense salaries whilst millions who contribute to these can hardly earn a living wage. Heads of companies draw huge salaries even when what they are managing is making suicidal losses. "Celebrities" are happy to be given the blasphemous status of idols.
- Perversion is a strong word, and it is not for any one of us to make personal condemnations; we are all sinners. It is neither a case of attitude or prejudice, but one of faith and conviction. God has made certain truths clear, and more stable society results from observing them: *"So God created man in his own image, in the image of God created he him; male and female created he them"* (Gen 1:27). Gen 19:1-29; Lev 20:13, Judg 19:20-23, Rom 1:26-32 testify to the same truth. When so-called Christian denominations openly defy God in these matters, they invite judgment.
- "Positive initiatives" as, when on a single day (5th April 2017), the Pope welcomed three British imams and a multi-faith service was held in the Anglican Westminster Abbey; the secular world applauded.
- National administrations, having rejected God, are facing such leadership crises and insuperable problems, that one can more than ever before visualise their future welcoming of Satan's coming strong man or "Man of Sin", whatever the cost.
- Witchcraft and Voodooism increasingly regarded as harmless alternatives to Christianity.

4.d. LUKE-WARMNESS WITHIN CHURCHES:
- Ephesian type churches (Rev 2:1-7), full of activities, but with their first love having departed.
- Laodicean type pride (Rev 3:14-21) in unspiritual

congregations with high opinions of themselves and the Lord outside seeking entrance.
- Scoffing, apathy and downright ignorance regarding the Lord's Return.
- A watered down Gospel with the 'threat' removed and central doctrines marginalised.
- Reversal of the great spiritual recoveries of the costly Reformation.
- Worldliness within the Church, blurred distinctions, lack of separation.
- Friendly overtures towards other faiths.
- Frenzied, repetitive worship almost indistinguishable from entertainment.
- Church attendances in Britain halved within last thirty years, and Sunday school membership very much more greatly reduced in aging congregations.
- False prophecies of impending spiritual prosperity within mainstream Christianity discredited by their failure to materialise.
- Occult manifestations such as the "Toronto Blessing" defying Scriptural guidelines.
- Self esteem, self-aggrandisement and personal salvation replacing humility.
- "Faith in faith" and the "power of prayer" being promoted, regardless of who these are directed towards.
- "Positive thinking" and such psychological gimmicks replacing repentance as a precursor to new life in Christ.

2017 Up-Date:
- Steady intensification and acceleration of all the above as the day draws nigh.
- Presentation of "inclusiveness" and "diversity" as Christian virtues, irrespective of who or what is included, effectively implying God's love of sin as well as of the sinner.
- New "politically correct" version Bibles now in use in some denominations, with deliberate distortions of the

Part One - The Facts Of The Second Coming

Word of God, and gender-specific statements being rendered as gender-neutral.
- More commitment to "saving the planet" and carbon footprints than filling our great commission and preaching the Gospel and saving souls.
- Churches worthy of God's rebuke to Job: *"Shall the one who contends with the Almighty correct Him? He who rebukes God, let him answer it......"Would you indeed annul My judgment? Would you condemn Me that you may be justified?* (Job 40:2,8) (NKJV). This is precisely what church men and women dare to do today.
- Sexual abuse against children and other vulnerable people within Christian institutes and organisations.

4.e. ISRAEL IN THE EYE OF THE STORM
- Israel's as yet incomplete return to the Promised Land after almost nineteen centuries.
- The rebirth of a long dead language - Hebrew.
- Israel's survival against overwhelming military odds in 1948, 1967 and since, making a mockery of the rhetoric of Islam and exposing the falsehoods of the Koran and Islamic prophecy.
- Israel already viewed as a *"burdensome stone"* for all nations, as prophesied by Zechariah.
- Palestinians clamouring for a two nations state, whilst making no secret of the fact that they would if possible annihilate Israel, should this be achieved
- Jerusalem still trodden underfoot by the Gentiles, as per Jesus' timescale.
- Centrally located among currently the most belligerent of modern nations.

2017 Up-Date:
- Greatly increased warfare and destruction in Israel's immediate neighbour, Syria, with limited military involvement of the major nations, with or without vested interests. Some of these nations feature in the future

- abortive end-time invasion of Israel foretold by Ezekiel – see Section 17.
- Further international isolation, with even the United States of America, long Israel's most loyal supporter, considering a two nation (Israeli and Palestinian) status. This was the policy of the losing 2016 presidential candidate. Did God overrule?
- Temporary partial diversion of international attention from Israel to squabbling neighbours very fragile.
- Further comments will be given in Sections 15 and 17.

The vast majority of the above are attributable directly or indirectly to human action, often prompted by *"the rulers of the darkness of this world"*. Paul reminds us that *"we wrestle not against flesh and blood, but against principalities, against powers, against the rulers of the darkness of this world, against spiritual wickedness in high places"* (Eph 6:12). Believers have always been involved in spiritual warfare. When they have failed to meet the challenge, as they have often done, they face defeat. Now in the 21st Century some are not only running away; many professing Christians in major denominations are defecting to the enemy, rejecting God's laws and embracing the enemy's. Let us take very seriously indeed Jesus' warning: *"When these things begin to come to pass, then look up, and lift up your heads; for your redemption draweth nigh"* (Lk 21:28).

PART TWO

BIBLICAL EVIDENCE AND BRIEF OVERVIEW OF THE END TIMES

5. THE MIRACLE OF PREDICTIVE PROPHECY

Having in the four previous sections summarised most of what is implied in the title of this book, namely certain key questions regarding Christ's Second Coming, God's right to intervene and the reasons for increased urgency, we can afford to devote a little space to background topics for those who wish to refer to any or all of them. A brief single page chronological table of the main events referred to in this book, past present and future, can be found after the final section for ease of reference. At the time of Christ's First Coming, apathy towards God's promises abounded and people clung to the status quo. Today, as the Second Coming draws ever closer, these same features abound within the religious community. We need to understand why.

We are creatures of time; we are used to a three dimensional universe and feel comfortable with it. We find it virtually impossible to comprehend timelessness. We read in Hebrews 1:2 that God *"Hath in these last days spoken unto us by his Son, whom he hath appointed heir of all things, by whom also he made the worlds"*. A better rendering is: *"through whom also He did make the ages"* (Young's Literal Translation). The Greek word is *aion*, and means just that. The point is that God created time and is in total control of it! God's knowledge of the future is as accurate as it is of the past or present.

Some Bible prophecies are conditional. They relate to what God has said would happen if people did or did not do certain things.

But here we are concerned with His unconditional prophecies, of which there are numerous, both in the Old and New Testaments. There are around three hundred and thirty in the Old Testament referring to Christ's First Coming; all were fulfilled, although sometimes one has to take two or more together to perceive this. God held responsible the vast majority of the Jewish religious leaders, who deliberately ignored them and brought the inevitable consequences upon themselves and their nation.

One feature which Old Testament readers had to face is that often prophecies referring to Christ's First and Second Comings have no apparent break between them. Only from a New Testament perspective can we see where a break of perhaps two thousand years occurs. One might reasonably say that they were not meant to perceive such a break, and that this lack of a break was deliberate Divine policy. That is because Jews were to be given by God the genuine option of accepting their Messiah at His First Coming, although in His wisdom He knew that they would reject it! There are two independent truths here, difficult for us creatures of time to comprehend. Many Old Testament end-time (unfulfilled future) prophecies can be fitted into a coherent pattern only in the light of the New Testament and with careful study.

It is a sad reflection that we find in appendices to some Bibles lists of "Messianic prophecies" which actually end with Christ's Ascension, forty days after His resurrection. Yet we find the eleven Apostles asking a very reasonable question: *"When they therefore were come together, they asked of him, saying, Lord, wilt thou at this time restore again the kingdom to Israel? And he said unto them, It is not for you to know the times or the seasons, which the Father hath put in his own power"* (Acts 1:6-7). They were referring to a well-known Messianic prophecy, and Jesus did not dismiss their question; it was merely not pertinent at that time. Immediately after their Lord ascended to Heaven they were given by angels a further Messianic promise: *"And while*

Part Two - Biblical Evidence And Brief Overview Of The End Times

they looked stedfastly toward heaven as he went up, behold, two men stood by them in white apparel; Which also said, Ye men of Galilee, why stand ye gazing up into heaven? this same Jesus, which is taken up from you into heaven, shall so come in like manner as ye have seen him go into heaven" (Acts 1:10-11). We refer to these important prophecies again.

Both Paul and Peter in their epistles give us important prophecies, but most predictive prophetic coverage is to be found in the Book of Revelation. It opens with the words: *"The Revelation of Jesus Christ, which God gave unto him, to shew unto his servants things which must shortly come to pass."* The word translated "shortly" can also indicate "quickly" or "in quick succession". The first three chapters contain serious messages from the risen Lord to believers in seven actual congregations, which typify others down through the subsequent ages. From Chapter 4 on we are given a record of John's vision of the future, written in a way which allows us to understand the salient features, even of that part which relates to what John saw as due to happen in Heaven. In fact no other book in the Bible is so solemnly introduced, claiming our attention. Revelation is the only book in the Bible with Christ's personal foreword: *"Blessed is he that readeth, and they that hear the words of this prophecy, and keep those things which are written therein: for the time is at hand"* (1:3). Here are Christ's last recorded public statements and messages to the world before His Second Coming.

We must concede that there are many visions in Revelation which are hard to visualise or interpret; but what we must never do is to underestimate the severity, intensity or scale of what is described. They are prophecies, not object lessons. God does not exaggerate! No other book has such dire warnings of meddling with its contents. Yet thousands of theologians ignore, trivialise or allegorise it. God is aware of such evasive practices, and records Ezekiel's justified complaint when he was giving straightforward predictions: *"Then said I, Ah Lord GOD! they say of me, Doth he not speak parables?"* (Ezek 20:49). John might have said the same had he been aware of 21st Century approaches to Revelation.

Jesus' prophetic Olivet Discourse, of which we have more to say at Section 9, is rarely if ever touched on from the pulpit or platform. It is all very well for congregations to repeat weekly *"Thy Kingdom come on earth, as it is in Heaven"*. Yet it is often recited as if it has no conceivable bearing upon current world events! Jesus was not telling us to pray for something unobtainable; in Section 18 we will see how this aspiration will eventually be answered to that exacting Heaven-like standard!

Much of this vagueness can be traced back to the 4th Century and Augustine of Hippo and contemporaries, who decreed that all Scripture should be taken literally, except prophecy, which should be interpreted allegorically. They dare to call this 'spiritualising', suggesting something praiseworthy. Were we to apply the same principle to First Coming prophecies, we would be left without a Gospel to preach. In Section 18 we will look briefly at the scoffing attitudes to Christ's Second Coming which were prophesied for the last days by Peter (II Pet 3:3-4).

A further significant problem among many generally Bible believing Christians is that they assume Christ's Second Coming to be a single event, unlike His First Coming. The result is that they find it impossible to fit a wide variety of prophecies into this supposed single event and give up. We consider this in Section 8.

A strange phenomenon of the latter half of the 20th century, which might be described as a false dawn, caused considerable damage, because it dashed the hopes of some who had been prematurely elated, resulting in what one might term spiritual casualties. Many Christians at that time proclaimed loudly (and sang loudly too!) that the Church was marching forward triumphantly and taking over the world prior to Christ's Return. It was a nice idea, but totally at odds with what Jesus Himself and the prophets had predicted.

Part Two - Biblical Evidence And Brief Overview Of The End Times

Some use the excuse that some prophecy is couched in poetic language, so need not be taken literally. While some is indeed recorded in poetic language, the majority is not. Often those poetic passages describe the almighty acts of God, past present and future, which would be beyond our comprehension if recorded in plain language. That does not make them any less meaningful.

A world in escalating crisis has been foretold in the Bible. Whatever our race, gender, social class and political views, we should all be concerned. As we shall be reminded in the final section, there are clear and simple steps which we can take, not to halt the inevitable, but to be personally prepared and secure in our relationship with God.

6. OLD TESTAMENT END-TIME PROPHECIES

Here are some important unconditional end-time prophecies from the Old Testament. I am making no comment about them at this juncture.

Some of the following quotes we will return to later. I have dealt with these at greater length with varying emphases in other books. Please remember that, while in this section I am quoting only unfulfilled Old Testament prophecies, these are frequently interspersed with First Coming ones in the text. Here I am presenting them roughly in expected order of fulfilment, allowing for some obvious overlap:-

- *"The LORD said unto my Lord, Sit thou at my right hand, until I make thine enemies thy footstool"* (Ps 110:1).
- *"Ask ye now, and see whether a man doth travail with child? wherefore do I see every man with his hands on his loins, as a woman in travail, and all faces are turned into paleness?"* (Jer 30:6).
- *"And at that time shall Michael stand up, the great prince which standeth for the children of thy people* (Daniel's people, Israel)*: and there shall be a time of trouble, such as never was since there was a nation even to that same*

- *time: and at that time thy people shall be delivered, every one that shall be found written in the book"* (Dan 12:1).
- *"The earth is utterly broken down, the earth is clean dissolved, the earth is moved exceedingly. The earth shall reel to and fro like a drunkard, and shall be removed like a cottage"* (Isa 24:19-20).
- *"For, behold, the LORD will come with fire, and with his chariots like a whirlwind, to render his anger with fury, and his rebuke with flames of fire"* (Isa 66:15).
- *For, behold, the day cometh, that shall burn as an oven; and all the proud, yea, and all that do wickedly, shall be stubble: and the day that cometh shall burn them up, saith the LORD of hosts, that it shall leave them neither root nor branch. But unto you that fear my name shall the Sun of righteousness arise with healing in his wings"* (Mal 4:1-2).
- *"Yea, all kings shall fall down before him: all nations shall serve him"* (Ps 72:11).
- *"And he shall judge among many people, and rebuke strong nations afar off; and they shall beat their swords into plowshares, and their spears into pruninghooks: nation shall not lift up a sword against nation, neither shall they learn war any more"* (Mic 4:3).
- *"All nations whom thou hast made shall come and worship before thee, O Lord; and shall glorify thy name"* (Ps 86:9).
- *"And it shall come to pass, that every one that is left of all the nations which came against Jerusalem shall even go up from year to year to worship the King, the LORD of hosts, and to keep the feast of tabernacles"* (Zech 14:16)
- *"The wilderness and the solitary place shall be glad for them; and the desert shall rejoice, and blossom as the rose"* (Isa 35:1).
- *"For, behold, I create new heavens and a new earth: and the former shall not be remembered, nor come into mind"* (Isa 65:17).

We will encounter others as we proceed.

7. NEW TESTAMENT END-TIME PROPHECIES

On this occasion I am adding a few very brief comments.

No unconditional Old Testament prophecy is ever made void in the New Testament. I am placing these in a suggested order of fulfilment, again allowing for some overlap, rather than as they appear in the text. We will be returning to some later:-

- *"And they shall fall by the edge of the sword, and shall be led away captive into all nations: and Jerusalem shall be trodden down of the Gentiles, until the times of the Gentiles be fulfilled"* (Lk 21:24). This takes us from the 70 AD fall of Jerusalem to a future date.
- *"In my Father's house are many mansions: if it were not so, I would have told you. I go to prepare a place for you. And if I go and prepare a place for you, I will come again, and receive you unto myself; that where I am, there ye may be also"* (Jn 14:2-3). Believers' souls have been in a 'mansion' or resting place in the Father's House (Heaven) since death
- *"For if we believe that Jesus died and rose again, even so them also which sleep in Jesus will God bring with him. For this we say unto you by the word of the Lord, that we which are alive and remain unto the coming of the Lord shall not prevent them which are asleep. For the Lord himself shall descend from heaven with a shout, with the voice of the archangel, and with the trump of God: and the dead in Christ shall rise first: Then we which are alive and remain shall be caught up together with them in the clouds, to meet the Lord in the air: and so shall we ever be with the Lord"* (I Thess 4:14-17). We will go through this passage step by step in Section 10.
- *"Behold, I shew you a mystery; We shall not all sleep, but we shall all be changed, In a moment, in the twinkling of an eye, at the last trump: for the trumpet shall sound,*

- *and the dead shall be raised incorruptible, and we shall be changed"* (I Cor 15:51-52).
- *"And ye shall hear of wars and rumours of wars: see that ye be not troubled: for all these things must come to pass, but the end is not yet. For nation shall rise against nation* (or *ethnic group against ethnic group*), *and kingdom against kingdom: and there shall be famines, and pestilences, and earthquakes, in divers places. All these are the beginning of sorrows"* (birth pains) (Matt 24:6-7).
- *"For then shall be great tribulation, such as was not since the beginning of the world to this time, no, nor ever shall be"* (Matt 24:21).
- **And I saw when the Lamb opened one of the seals, and I heard, as it were the noise of thunder, one of the four beasts saying, Come and see"* (Rev 6:1). The consecutive opening of the seven seals is followed by ominous happenings on earth – see Section 13.
- *"And I saw the seven angels which stood before God; and to them were given seven trumpets"* (Rev 8:2). Each trumpet blast is followed by a catastrophic event upon earth – see Section13.
- *And I stood upon the sand of the sea, and saw a beast rise up out of the sea, having seven heads and ten horns, and upon his horns ten crowns, and upon his heads the name of blasphemy* (Rev 13:1). This Beast, Man of Sin or final Antichrist is to dominate world events during the Tribulation Period – see Section 14 for this and the following three bullet points.
- *And I beheld another beast coming up out of the earth; and he had two horns like a lamb, and he spake as a dragon"* (Rev 13:11). This is the False Prophet, who, along with the Devil and First Beast, parody the Holy Trinity.
- *And he causeth all, both small and great, rich and poor, free and bond, to receive a mark in their right hand, or in their foreheads: And that no man might buy or sell,*

save he that had the mark, or the name of the beast, or the number of his name" (Rev 13:16-17). Acceptance of this Mark of the Beast indicates submission to and willing worship of Satan.

- *"And the third angel followed them, saying with a loud voice, If any man worship the beast and his image, and receive his mark in his forehead, or in his hand, the same shall drink of the wine of the wrath of God, which is poured out without mixture into the cup of his indignation; and he shall be tormented with fire and brimstone in the presence of the holy angels, and in the presence of the Lamb"* (Rev 14:9-10). But of course God is to offer an infinitely better alternative!
- *"And this gospel of the kingdom shall be preached in all the world for a witness unto all nations; and then shall the end come"* (Matt 24:14). This is to be truly global..
- "*And I saw another angel fly in the midst of heaven, having the everlasting gospel to preach unto them that dwell on the earth, and to every nation, and kindred, and tongue, and people, Saying with a loud voice, Fear God, and give glory to him; for the hour of his judgment is come: and worship him that made heaven, and earth, and the sea, and the fountains of waters"* (Rev 14:6-7). Even in earth's darkest hour God will ensure that the gospel will be preached and every opportunity will be given for repentance and salvation, although this may involve persecution or death.
- *And I heard a great voice out of the temple saying to the seven angels, Go your ways, and pour out the vials of the wrath of God upon the earth"* (Rev 16:1). Vials are bowls. These are the cataclysmic final judgments of the Great Tribulation; they occur in quick succession and affect the whole earth – see Section 13.
- *"They are the spirits of demons, working miracles, which go forth unto the kings of the earth and of the whole world, to gather them to the battle of that great day of God Almighty….. And he gathered them together into a place*

- *called in the Hebrew tongue Armageddon"* (Rev 16:14 &16) – see Sections 11 & 14 for this and the following four bullet points.
- *"Ye men of Galilee, why stand ye gazing up into heaven? this same Jesus, which is taken up from you into heaven, shall so come in like manner as ye have seen him go into heaven"* (Acts 1:11)
- *"Behold, he cometh with clouds; and every eye shall see him, and they also which pierced him: and all kindreds of the earth shall wail because of him"* (Rev 1:7).
- *"And I saw heaven opened, and behold a white horse; and he that sat upon him was called Faithful and True, and in righteousness he doth judge and make war..... And the armies which were in heaven followed him upon white horses, clothed in fine linen, white and clean"* (Rev19:11 &14).
- *"And I saw the beast, and the kings of the earth, and their armies, gathered together to make war against him that sat on the horse, and against his army. And the beast was taken, and with him the false prophet that wrought miracles before him, with which he deceived them that had received the mark of the beast, and them that worshipped his image. These both were cast alive into a lake of fire burning with brimstone"* (Rev 19:19-20).
- *"When the Son of man shall come in his glory, and all the holy angels with him, then shall he sit upon the throne of his glory: And before him shall be gathered all nations: and he shall separate them one from another, as a shepherd divideth his sheep from the goats"* (Matt 25:31-32) – see Section 17 for this and the next bullet point..
- *"Lo, a great multitude, which no man could number, of all nations, and kindreds, and people, and tongues, stood before the throne, and before the Lamb, clothed with white robes, and palms in their hands..... These are they which came out of great tribulation, and have washed their robes, and made them white in the blood of the*

Lamb" (Rev 7:9 & 14). These are the ones likened to sheep at the Judgment of the Nations (Matt 25:31-46).

8. THE DURATION OF CHRIST'S FIRST AND SECOND COMINGS

If we remind ourselves that Christ's First Coming extended over three and a half decades, we will be less tempted to think of His Second Coming as a single event. Christ came from Heaven, to which, only after completing His mission, He returned. So very much happened between His arrival and departure, as recorded in the four Gospels. John commented: *"And many other signs truly did Jesus in the presence of his disciples, which are not written in this book"* (Jn 20:30)

Christ's First Coming commenced with what we call His incarnation, or taking a human form, without relinquishing His Godhood. John is privileged to record Jesus' prayer: *"And now, O Father, glorify thou me with thine own self with the glory which I had with thee before the world was"* (Jn 17:5). John also writes: *"And the Word was made flesh, and dwelt among us"* (Jn 1:14). Jesus Christ became incarnate – took on human flesh - not in Bethlehem, but when Gabriel's prophecy to Mary was fulfilled: *"The Holy Ghost shall come upon thee, and the power of the Highest shall overshadow thee: therefore also that holy thing which shall be born of thee shall be called the Son of God"* (Lk 1:35). Mary met John the Baptist's mother, and it is recorded: *"When Elisabeth heard the salutation of Mary, the babe leaped in her womb; and Elisabeth was filled with the Holy Ghost"* (Lk 1:41). People may talk of embryos and foetuses, but in our Creator's eyes, these were unborn babies. Formerly Christian nations can be held accountable for turning their backs on such clear revelations of God.

His First Coming became public at His baptism, where He was identified by John the Baptist as *"The Lamb of God, which taketh away the sin of the world"* (Jn 1:29), and His public ministry commenced in His home synagogue where He made what is

Christ's Second Coming

sometimes called His mission statement, as related at Lk 4:16-21: *"The Spirit of the Lord is upon me, because he hath anointed me to preach the gospel to the poor; he hath sent me to heal the brokenhearted, to preach deliverance to the captives, and recovering of sight to the blind, to set at liberty them that are bruised….."* These were of course immensely important events, but they neither introduced nor closed His First Coming.

Three years later He formally presented Himself to His city of Jerusalem, in fulfilment of Zechariah's famous (9:9) prophecy: *"Rejoice greatly, O daughter of Zion; shout, O daughter of Jerusalem: behold, **thy King cometh** unto thee: he is just, and having salvation; lowly, and riding upon an ass, and upon a colt the foal of an ass"* (Zech 9:9). That also was a highly significant part of His First Coming.

Now of course Jesus had already forewarned His disciples that Jerusalem's citizens would reject Him. In effect it was the city's reaction which determined that only after a long delay will He eventually return to that same city, and be welcomed. Jesus warned Jerusalem: *For I say unto you, Ye shall not see me henceforth, till ye shall say, Blessed is he that cometh in the name of the Lord.* (Matt 23:39)..That condition has yet to be fulfilled. What was their loss has proved to be our gain. In the meantime Jerusalem and the nation of which she was capital have been side-lined in God's purposes, and the Church, consisting almost entirely of Gentiles or non-Jews has been responsible for representing God to the world. This she has not always done adequately; perhaps her time is drawing to a close. Simon Peter explained the transfer of responsibility in Acts 15:11-18. *"Simon has declared how God at the first visited the Gentiles to take out of them a people for His name. And with this the words of the prophets agree, just as it is written: 'After this I will return and will rebuild the tabernacle of David, which has fallen down; I will rebuild its ruins"* (vv 14-16 NKJV). The reassuring comment is then made: *"Known to God from eternity are all His works"* (Acts 15:18 NKJV). Jerusalem's rejection was

Part Two - Biblical Evidence And Brief Overview Of The End Times

no accident of history, neither was the Church an afterthought or a "New Israel". The spiritually restored old Israel still features in God's revealed plans.

We have seen that many events fitted in sequence into Christ's First Coming. We should therefore find it easy to appreciate that a sequence of events over a period of time is predicted for His Second Coming. However, in many churches Christ's Second Coming is condensed into very brief statements and rarely expanded. The Nicene Creed of 325 AD, up-dated in 381 and still in use, simply says: *"(He) ascended into heaven, and sitteth on the right hand of the Father, and He shall come again with glory to judge both the quick and the dead; Whose Kingdom shall have no end."* The later so-called Apostles' Creed is even briefer. The impression thus given and firmly imprinted on all too many minds is that a final single judgment is to follow the Lord's Second Coming. That is very different from what Jesus' Olivet Discourse, the Book of Revelation and many other passages teach.

Let me make it quite clear that seeing the Second Coming as a single event does not constitute some form of apostasy or heresy. I know many fine believers who see it as a single event. On the other hand I have to concede that the amount of time they spend studying His Second Coming bears no relation to the proportion of space which Scripture, including the recorded words of the Lord Himself, allocates to it. The sad result is that, when this happens at leadership level within a congregation, as it does frequently, members are left with the woolliest ideas about the afterlife, Heaven and Hell, and are unable to contend with the cults or even adequately counsel the bereaved, which is a shameful situation.

Back at Sections 6 and 7 I quoted, with minimum comment, a number of the best known end-time prophecies. There is surely something far wrong if we are unable to see a coherent pattern. More and more, as I encounter people who stick most rigidly to the single event Second Coming of the Creeds, I am convinced that this tunnel vision is the major cause for inability to see a coherent pattern, and of resultant apathy. We return to this briefly at Section 18.

9. THE SEQUENCE OF EVENTS AT CHRIST'S SECOND COMING

It might be helpful to remind ourselves what happens to the individual at death, without going into details. The body dies and suffers corruption in one form or other. God who created DNA can be trusted to ensure that at the appropriate time there will be a resurrection of the same individual but in a glorious incorruptible form; I Cor 15:35-38 summarised the process eloquently nineteen centuries before DNA was identified by scientists. The soul of the believer goes immediately in a conscious state to a dwelling place, occasionally referred to as Paradise (Lk 23:43), in the Father's House to await the First Resurrection, which will comprise the *"redemption of the body"* (Rom 8:23). The soul of the unbeliever goes to a conscious state to Sheol or Hades (the Old and New Testament names) to await the Second Resurrection. Thus death is the temporary separation of the soul from the body, whilst the resurrection is the reunification.

I propose to look in the next section at what we might call "The Opening Event of Christ's Second Coming", and then leap forward in the following section to what we might call the "Climactic Event of Christ's Second Coming". I believe that this will be helpful, because so much confusion arises through people trying to rationalise and condense into a single event what the Bible presents as two contrasting events. Only then, in Sections 12 and 13, will I take time to summarise what is to happen both in Heaven and upon earth between the Opening and Climactic events.

Periodically I refer to Jesus' Olivet Discourse. A few brief comments might be helpful for any who wish to explore further. Much the greatest coverage of the Discourse is found in Matthew

Part Two - Biblical Evidence And Brief Overview Of The End Times

chapters 24 and 25, but parts are also recorded in Mark 13 and Luke 21. Jesus was addressing Jewish believers before the nation's final rejection: *"But they cried out, Away with him, away with him, crucify him. Pilate saith unto them, Shall I crucify your King? The chief priests answered, We have no king but Caesar"* (Jn 19:15). Therefore, while the Discourse is there for the information of all believers, and to alert Church Age believers to the signs of the times, it is primarily **about** Israel's future within the world scenario. Luke 21:5-24 records what was to happen up to and including the sacking of Jerusalem in 70 AD and the start of the long dispersal or *diaspora*, before adding a little about the End Times from verse 25. Matthew 24 from verse 4 to 44 deals with events around the return from the *diaspora* and the ultra-traumatic period immediately before and during Christ's return to earth (see Sections 11 & 17). Then follow three relevant parables (24:45 – 25:30), before we are told of an important segregating event immediately following that return to earth (25:31-46) – see Section 18.

From New Testament times there have been earnest admonitions for us constantly to be ready for Christ's Second Coming, and yet there are clearly to be a number of momentous events which are predicted to occur before His coming **to earth**. This is an enigma until one appreciates that **there are no specific preconditions for the Opening Event, but powerful preconditions for the Climactic Event.** As far as we are concerned, the Opening Event could occur at any second.

10. THE OPENING EVENT OF CHRIST'S SECOND COMING

One cannot over-emphasis the fact that we are given no data for calculating the end of the present Church Age. *"But of that day and hour knoweth no man, no, not the angels of heaven, but my Father only"* (Matt 24:36); whilst on earth He left such matters in His Father's hands. Now, as we have just observed, Jesus had been addressing His own nation in His Olivet Discourse; Israel is to undergo the Tribulation Period which is to follow the Church

Age, as we will be reminded at Section 17. When Jesus spoke, the Church and Church Age had yet to be born on the Day of Pentecost. Jesus left it to the writers of the Epistles to foretell His later return for His Church, at what we sometimes call the Rapture, from the Latin word for *"to catch up"*. Jesus knew that these passages would be read frequently during the Church Age, when the Rapture would be the immediate goal of believers. He must also have known that they would also be read by Jews and others during the Tribulation period following the Rapture, when His Coming in Power or climactic event would become the juncture which suffering believers would be desperately longing for. Thus they are relevant to both groups of believers.

What I want to demonstrate briefly is the marked contrast between the opening and later events of Christ's Second Coming. We will see why the Church is to *wait* for her *Lord*, whereas Israel is to *watch* for the *Son of Man*. The only direct reference to the Rapture in the Gospels (as opposed to the Church epistles) is contained in Jn 14:2-3, where Jesus was talking exclusively to believers. He had already prepared them for His crucifixion and resurrection; now He was preparing them for His ascension and what was to follow: *"In my Father's house are many mansions* (dwelling places or similar in other translations)*: if it were not so, I would have told you. I go to prepare a place for you. And if I go and prepare a place for you, I will come again, and receive you unto myself; that where I am, there ye may be also"* (Jn 14:2-3). The Paradise where Jesus promised the penitent thief that they both would be that very day (just before sunset) already existed in the Father's House. Of course Jesus' soul remained there only from His death until the dawn of the third day, whilst the thief remains there awaiting his resurrection.

So, while there are already many occupied resting places in Heaven, the place Jesus was going to prepare after His Ascension is as yet unoccupied. It is likened to the bridal home of resurrected believers. Jesus on that occasion (Jn 14:1-3) was not talking about His "coming **to**", but about His "coming

for". The Greek preposition is very clear. When He comes in power and glory He will "come **to**". He left it to Paul to describe that future event. The two main Rapture passages have already been quoted at Section 7; let us now requote them sentence by sentence with brief comments. We start with I Thess 4:17-18:-

- *"For if we believe that Jesus died and rose again, even so them also which sleep in Jesus will God bring with him."* These are the **souls** of those who sleep in Christ, conscious and at peace in Heaven. He is going to bring these souls with Him to the meeting point with their newly raised **bodies**. This is therefore their awaited resurrection.
- *"For this we say unto you by the word of the Lord."* Paul was especially commissioned to reveal this information to the young Church.
- *"that we which are alive and remain unto the coming of the Lord shall not prevent* ('precede' in most versions) *them which are asleep."* Thus believers still alive on earth up to this point will not die.
- *"For the Lord himself shall descend from heaven with a shout, with the voice of the archangel, and with the trump of God"*
- *"and the dead in Christ shall rise first."* This is the main part (or main harvest) of the first resurrection. No mention is made here of unbelievers.
- *"then we which are alive and remain shall be caught up together with them in the clouds, to meet the Lord in the air".* The meeting point of resurrected and raptured living believers is to be out of sight of earth, hidden by clouds, the parting point of Jesus' ascension so long ago.
- *"and so shall we ever be with the Lord."* Together resurrected and never-having-died believers, who will now constitute the complete Church, are taken to the place which He went to prepare. When He leaves Heaven to return to earth a little later, we must follow Him, along with the angelic army. Humans of course never turn into angels; that is a myth.

We now turn to I Cor 15:51-52 for a little supplementary information about this stupendous event:-
- *"Behold, I shew you a mystery;"* This had to wait until the post-Pentecost Church Age to be revealed; it is no longer a mystery.
- *We shall not all sleep, but we shall all be changed,"* "All" – Paul was addressing ordinary members of the Corinthian congregation – there is no selection, segregation or separation of believers.
- *In a moment, in the twinkling of an eye, at the last trump."* The last trumpet blast (usually one of three, as with the Children of Israel at the Exodus), is the march off call. *"for the trumpet shall sound, and the dead shall be raised incorruptible".* It is the wake-up call for those who have suffered the corruption of the body in death. It is not to be confused with the last of seven trumpet blasts for judgment in Revelation. The glorious new bodies, adapted for Heaven and eternity, will be incorruptible.
- *"and we shall be changed."* Those believers caught up alive, irrespective of age, gender, physical condition, race etc will be wonderfully transformed without dying.

It is important that we should understand this. Only the *"dead in Christ"* and living believers will participate in the Rapture. Remember that, at the Rapture, Jesus Christ is returning as the heavenly Bridegroom FOR His Bride, the Church. The Church is seen as the Bride of the Lamb collectively, not individually. In the later climactic event He will return WITH His Bride. I quote briefly from my *"Rapture Sooner Not Later"* with added comments. Contemporary Jewish marriage customs are often referred to in the New Testament, from the Gospels through to Revelation, and prophetically from Matthew 25:1 onwards. The custom was that the bridegroom:-
- Paid the bride-price, consecrating his betrothed to himself. (This Jesus did at Calvary).
- Returned to the father's home to prepare a place for her. (This Jesus did at His Ascension).

- Came back, often suddenly, usually at midnight, to claim his bride, whom he would take to his father's house, where the marriage would be consummated. (This Jesus will do at the Rapture).
- Returned to the bride's original home, where those invited by the bridegroom's father would be waiting for the wedding feast. (This He will do at the climactic event which we will look at shortly).

Christ is going to take His Bride home before the coming wrath – the Tribulation period. We are to *"wait for his Son **from** heaven, whom he raised **from** the dead, even Jesus, which delivered us **from** the wrath to come"* (I Thess 1:10). The Greek preposition for 'from' in the first two instances is *ek,* indicating "out of", but the third is *apo,* meaning "away from". Had the third been *ek,* it would have indicated that the Church is to go through the Tribulation, but as it is, it is going to be taken away first. *"For God hath not appointed us to wrath, but to obtain salvation by our Lord Jesus Christ"* (I Thess 5:9).

The sudden disappearance of what one can reasonably assume to be hundreds of millions of believers will inevitably throw the world into a crisis, though we suspect, but cannot prove, that God will miraculously overrule to ensure that millions of accidents do not result from suddenly driverless vehicles and pilotless aircraft etc. In Sections 13 and 14 we shall see how Satan will exploit this crisis for his own short-term advantage.

The Bible does not tell us about children at the Rapture, although the youngest **believing** child will certainly be raptured in his or her own right as part of the Church. It seems almost certain that children of believers, and possibly even of non-believers, below the age of discretion (which God alone knows), will be taken to Heaven rather than left parentless to face the Tribulation. Jesus' declaration, *"It is not the will of your Father which is in heaven, that one of these little ones should perish"* (Matt 18:14), can probably be applied here, though we cannot be emphatic.

Here are a few other references to the Rapture:-
- *"For our conversation is in heaven; from whence also we look for the Saviour, the Lord Jesus Christ: Who shall change our vile body, that it may be fashioned like unto his glorious body, according to the working whereby he is able even to subdue all things unto himself"* (Phil 3:20-21).
- *"So Christ was once offered to bear the sins of many; and unto them that look for him shall he appear the second time without sin unto salvation"* (Heb 9:28).
- *"And when the chief Shepherd shall appear, ye shall receive a crown of glory that fadeth not away"* (I Pet 5:4).
- *"Beloved, now are we the sons of God, and it doth not yet appear what we shall be: but we know that, when he shall appear, we shall be like him; for we shall see him as he is"* (I Jn 3:2).
- *"Because thou hast kept the word of my patience, I also will keep thee from the hour of temptation, which shall come upon all the world, to try them that dwell upon the earth"* (Rev 3:10).

See also I Tim 6:14-15, Jas 5:8-9, I Jn 2:28.

11. THE CLIMACTIC EVENT OF CHRIST'S SECOND COMING

I call this section the Climactic Event rather than the closing event, because, as we shall see at Section 19, it not only closes the Day of Vengeance, but also inaugurates on earth the Millennial Kingdom or "Year of the Lord's Redeemed".

Now we are going to return to a few of the verses quoted back at the list of New Testament end-time prophecies. It is worth pausing to consider two contrasting statements which some may find confusing: *"Lo, I am with you always, even to the end of the age"* (Matt 28:20 NKJV) and *"That He may send Jesus Christ, who was preached to you before, "whom heaven must receive until the times of restoration of all things, which God has spoken by the mouth of all His holy prophets"* (Acts 3:20-21). We

Part Two - Biblical Evidence And Brief Overview Of The End Times

must remember that Jesus did not cease to be God when He became Man; therefore in this capacity He can be omnipresent – an exclusively Divine attribute – and thus present with all believers. But He did not cease to be Man when He ascended. Several times in the Olivet Discourse He emphasised that it will be as the Son of Man, in which capacity He has never returned to earth since His Ascension, that He will return in glory, as in: *"When the Son of man shall come in his glory, and all the holy angels with him, then shall he sit upon the throne of his glory"* (Matt 25:31).

This event is often referred to as His Coming in Power or Return in Power. The most detailed description is found in Revelation chapter 19. The scenario in Heaven immediately before this event is referred to in Section 12, and the scenario on earth in Section 13. It is the dramatic, glorious climactic event which we consider now. We can go through the main details step by step; there is endless scope for elaboration:-

- *"And I saw heaven opened, and behold a white horse; and he that sat upon him was called Faithful and True, and in righteousness he doth judge and make war. His eyes were as a flame of fire, and on his head were many crowns; and he had a name written, that no man knew, but he himself. And he was clothed with a vesture dipped in blood: and his name is called The Word of God"* (Rev 19:11-13). Heaven will be open to view; His exit from Heaven will be highly visible – compare with Jesus' own words: *"For as the lightning cometh out of the east, and shineth even unto the west; so shall also the coming of the Son of man be"* (Matt 24:27). The contrast with "Jehovah's Witnesses"' could not be greater. *"Behold, he cometh with clouds; and every eye shall see him, and they also which pierced him: and all kindreds of the earth shall wail because of him"* (Rev 1:7). How this will be accomplished we do not know, but it will be. Remember that souls of the unsaved awaiting resurrection are conscious and are not subject to time as we are.

- *"And the armies which were in heaven followed him upon white horses, clothed in fine linen, white and clean"* (Rev 19:14). We have already been reminded that the entire Church will have been resurrected and will already be in Heaven prior to this event. Jude tells us *"And Enoch also, the seventh from Adam, prophesied of these, saying, Behold, the Lord cometh with ten thousands of his saints, to execute judgment upon all"* (Jude 1:14-15). We have already seen that, from the Rapture onwards, *"we will ever be with our Lord"*, so it is only appropriate that we should follow Him.

- *"And out of his mouth goeth a sharp sword, that with it he should smite the nations: and he shall rule them with a rod of iron: and he treadeth the winepress of the fierceness and wrath of Almighty God"* (Rev 19:15). He is going both to smite as appropriate, and thereafter to rule autocratically, as is His right. This smiting is an act of judgment against those who have opposed Him. It would be worth reading the whole of Psalm 2 at this point, where we have recorded God the Father speaking to God the Son. We read: *"The kings of the earth set themselves, and the rulers take counsel together, against the LORD, and against his anointed, saying, Let us break their bands asunder, and cast away their cords from us"* (Ps 2:2-3). This is the ultimate, defiant open rebellion of the creature against the Creator. *"Ask of me, and I shall give thee the heathen for thine inheritance, and the uttermost parts of the earth for thy possession. Thou shalt break them with a rod of iron; thou shalt dash them in pieces like a potter's vessel"* (Ps 2:8-9). This is the Father's complete long-awaited public vindication of His Son, something held in abeyance on earth (as opposed to Heaven) since His humiliating death on the Cross.

- *"And he hath on his vesture and on his thigh a name written, KING OF KINGS, AND LORD OF LORDS"* (Rev

19:16). These are publicly displayed titles which He holds not because He is God, but because He became Man, and as such earned them.
- *"And I saw the beast, and the kings of the earth, and their armies, gathered together to make war against him that sat on the horse, and against his army"* (Rev 19:19). *"Then shall the LORD go forth, and fight against those nations, as when he fought in the day of battle. And his feet shall stand in that day upon the mount of Olives, which is before Jerusalem on the east, and the mount of Olives shall cleave in the midst thereof"* (Zech 14:3-4). He is to return in glory and victory to the very spot from which He ascended nearly two thousand years ago!
- *"And the beast was taken, and with him the false prophet that wrought miracles before him, with which he deceived them that had received the mark of the beast, and them that worshipped his image. These both were cast alive into a lake of fire burning with brimstone. And the remnant were slain with the sword of him that sat upon the horse, which sword proceeded out of his mouth: and all the fowls were filled with their flesh"* (Rev 19:20-21). *"And this shall be the plague wherewith the LORD will smite all the people that have fought against Jerusalem; Their flesh shall consume away while they stand upon their feet, and their eyes shall consume away in their holes, and their tongue shall consume away in their mouth"* (Zech 14:12). Zechariah describes the fate only of the human armies; Revelation also deals with the demonic elements.
- *"And I saw an angel come down from heaven, having the key of the bottomless pit and a great chain in his hand. And he laid hold on the dragon, that old serpent, which is the Devil, and Satan, and bound him a thousand years,* (Rev 20:1-2). The chapter break at the end of Revelation 19 is unfortunate – chapter divisions, which date only to the early days of printing, are often helpful, but are not inspired. However, as the continuous narrative then goes

on to tell of what happens immediately after the climactic event of Christ's Second Coming, we can now turn to what is to happen between these opening and climactic events. We have seen that all existing opposition will have been summarily dealt with at Christ's Coming in Power.

12. BETWEEN THE OPENING AND CLIMACTIC EVENTS – IN HEAVEN

Once in Heaven, we will be outside the realms of time – a situation difficult to conceive. Paul quotes Isaiah: *"Eye hath not seen, nor ear heard, neither have entered into the heart of man, the things which God hath prepared for them that love him"* (I Cor 2:9). But below on earth time will be ticking away, and we in Heaven will be aware of what is happening below, because we will be able to see for ourselves the heavenly controls being applied. The opposite will not of course be true, except on one occasion when God chooses to make it possible: *"And said to the mountains and rocks, Fall on us, and hide us from the face of him that sitteth on the throne, and from the wrath of the Lamb: For the great day of his wrath is come; and who shall be able to stand?"* (Rev 6:16-17).

The Apostle John, in the revelation of the future which the risen Christ gives him to record, having first passed on messages for existing congregations, relates: *"After this I looked, and, behold, a door was opened in heaven: and the first voice which I heard was as it were of a trumpet talking with me; which said, Come up hither, and I will shew thee things which must be hereafter. And immediately I was in the spirit: and, behold, a throne was set in heaven, and one sat on the throne"* (Rev 4:1-2). It is a vision in which we find that the risen Christ is in the midst of that throne. But John also sees "elders", who are unidentified, but are evidently prominent raptured saints; significantly they have just been awarded crowns, which they now proceed to cast before the One on the throne: *"The four and twenty elders fall down before him that sat on the throne, and worship him that liveth for ever and ever, and cast their crowns before the throne"* (Rev 4:10).

We are not given an eye-witness account of the prior awarding of these crowns, but we are told that we must all appear at a judgment, not of our sins, which were once and for all dealt with at Calvary and therefore cannot be punished, but of our works or service from the time we became believers. Paul tells us: *"We shall all stand before the judgment seat of Christ"* (Rom 14:10) and adds: *"For we must all appear before the judgment seat of Christ; that every one may receive the things done in his body, according to that he hath done, whether it be good or bad"* (II Cor 5:10). He likens the process to the metal refiner's fire, a familiar picture to his early readers: *"Every man's work shall be made manifest: for the day shall declare it, because it shall be revealed by fire; and the fire shall try every man's work of what sort it is. If any man's work abide which he hath built thereupon, he shall receive a reward. If any man's work shall be burned, he shall suffer loss: but he himself shall be saved; yet so as by fire"* (I Cor 3:13-15). It must be emphasised that this is no unscriptural Purgatory with its supposed physical pain – eternal destinations are sealed during this life; we are not here on probation with a second chance held in reserve. Apparently no believer will be left empty-handed: *"Every man shall receive his own reward according to his own labour"* (I Cor 3:8). Perhaps our minds are taken back to the well-known words of Jesus in His Sermon on the Mount: *"Lay up for yourselves treasures in heaven, where neither moth nor rust doth corrupt, and where thieves do not break through nor steal"* (Matt 6:20).

These are solemn matters, but they are worth recording, because some evangelists are so keen on stressing the key truth that our good deeds cannot get us into Heaven, that they forget that genuine service will not go unrewarded. Moreover such recognition is to be eternal! I Cor 9:25 tells us that these crowns will be incorruptible, not liable to fade like the familiar laurel wreaths awarded at Greek and Roman games.

Just before Christ's Return in power and glory, the Marriage of the Lamb will take place in Heaven. We considered this in the previous section, but we read: *"Let us be glad and rejoice, and give honour to him: for the marriage of the Lamb is come, and his wife hath made herself ready. And to her was granted that she should be arrayed in fine linen, clean and white: for the fine linen is the righteousness of saints"* (Rev 19:7-8). The relationship of the Church to the Lord Jesus Christ as the redeeming Lamb is unique and very precious.

I have included this section before looking at happenings upon earth between the opening and climactic events of Christ's Second Coming, because it explains and puts into perspective factors which otherwise might be confusing, such as:-

- The evident absence from the earth of the Church in Tribulation Period prophecy. The Church will be taken home rather than being side-lined on earth as was Israel of old.
- The Marriage of the Lamb in Heaven before His visible Return, something impossible without the prior completion of the Church and her appearance in Heaven.
- The sudden reappearance on earth of Jewish evangelists, and of Israel undergoing a final brief Holocaust and sifting, purging or refining, during the same period. I shall comment briefly how and why Israel fits so vividly into the picture in Sections 15 & 17.
- A period which ends, rather than begins, with *"except those days should be shortened, there should no flesh be saved: but for the elect's sake those days shall be shortened"*. That statement of Jesus follows His prediction: *"For then shall be great tribulation, such as was not since the beginning of the world to this time, no, nor ever shall be."*

Part Two - Biblical Evidence And Brief Overview Of The End Times

We can now review some of the contemporary earthly aspects.

13. BETWEEN THE OPENING AND CLIMACTIC EVENTS – ON EARTH

We now have a framework into which to fit some of the dramatic happenings on earth in the interval between the Rapture and Christ's Return in Power. Astonishingly, some assume that the Messianic mission of the Lord Jesus Christ, ended at His death, His resurrection or His ascension or, at the very latest, at Pentecost. In a sense it is a defeatist assumption, because it almost gives the impression that all that has happened in the world since then has been accidental, or at least incidental to God's plans and Bible prophecy. The fact is that the prophetic clock, so to speak, stopped ticking during the Church Age and will start again only after the Rapture. We will see further evidence at Section 16. A single important prophetic matter regarding the long interval or parenthesis is covered, not in the Church epistles, but in the Luke 21:5-24 section of Christ's Olivet Discourse, where it was highly appropriate. This is the brutal destruction of Jerusalem by the Romans in 70 AD, with the dispersal or *diaspora* of the inhabitants of Jerusalem and Judea, a dispersal which did not begin to be reversed until the Twentieth Century, when, still largely in unbelief, they began to return. How do we explain this Church Age vacuum of prophetic fulfilment?

We have noted that in the book of Isaiah there is a three stage sequence in the Messianic mission or programme:
- The Acceptable Year of the Lord
- The Day of Vengeance of our God
- The Year of the Lord's Redeemed

As in English, 'Year' and 'Day' in Old Testament Hebrew and New Testament Greek may apply to longer periods. When the two appear together, 'year' is invariably longer. Isaiah foretold that the coming Christ or Messiah would proclaim both: *"**The acceptable year of the LORD, and the day of vengeance of our God**"* (Isa 61:2).

Two chapters later Isaiah related a further Messianic statement, which includes the assurance of future comfort following suffering: *"For **the day of vengeance** is in mine heart, and **the year of my redeemed is come**"* (63:4). When Jesus first came and made His first public statement, in His local synagogue or place of worship, we find that He concluded His reading from Isaiah's scroll dramatically: *"To preach **the acceptable year of the Lord**. And he closed the book, and he gave it again to the minister, and sat down. And the eyes of all them that were in the synagogue were fastened on him"* (Lk 4:19-20). He emphatically did not cancel *"the day of vengeance of our God"*, but He did postpone it for many centuries. It still lies ahead. We are nearing the end of the Acceptable Year of the Lord, which is to terminate at the Rapture. The Day of Vengeance is to precede the Millennial Year of the Lord's Redeemed – the final stage of the Messianic mission, which is to conclude with: *"Then cometh the end, when he shall have delivered up the kingdom to God, even the Father; when he shall have put down all rule and all authority and power. For he must reign, till he hath put all enemies under his feet. The last enemy that shall be destroyed is death"* (I Cor 15:24-26).

Obviously thousands of millions will be left behind upon earth to endure the Day of Vengeance, the period of unprecedented tribulation upon earth. Satan, the *"father of lies"*, holds in reserve his Antichrist or false Christ, who will evidently come immediately to prominence after the Rapture, no doubt cleverly explaining the disappearance of the many millions of believers in a way which will suit his immediate purposes : *"And then shall that Wicked be revealed, whom the Lord shall consume with the spirit of his mouth, and shall destroy with the brightness of his coming: Even him, whose coming is after the working of Satan with all power and signs and lying wonders, and with all deceivableness of unrighteousness in them that perish; because they received not the love of the truth, that they might be saved. And for this cause God shall send them strong delusion, that they should believe a lie: that they all might be damned who believed not the truth,*

Part Two - Biblical Evidence And Brief Overview Of The End Times

but had pleasure in unrighteousness" (II Thess 2:8-12). We see more of this at Section 14. God is to permit this delusion for those who deserve to be deluded. We should be aware that we are not told the exact duration of the evidently short interval between the Rapture and the revelation of *"that Wicked". As we will be reminded in the next section, it* should not take Satan's Man of Sin long to establish himself in a world in unprecedented crisis.

We can speculate endlessly about how the sudden disappearance of millions of believers will be explained in this *"strong delusion".* Ingenious explanations and even novels have been written. It is something which no doubt Satan has had in mind ever since the Rapture was first announced around nineteen and a half centuries ago, so we may safely assume that it will be diabolically cunning and convincing for those who persist in rejecting God.

Certainly it appears from the II Thessalonians passage that those, who in this present Day of Grace have deliberately prevaricated or gambled with their eternal soul, will be unable to find repentance, even though a vast multitude of others will be able to later, as we shall see. We must not be tempted to think, as a few do, of the Tribulation period which is to follow the Rapture as a great adventure and challenge which it would be cowardly not to wish to live through. Just as God provided the Ark before the Flood for righteous Noah and his family, so Christ is going to take His Church home safe above what is raging below. Many will be saved after the Rapture, but they will be too late to be part of the Church. At Section 17 we will consider the evangelists who will preach the Gospel of the Kingdom at that time.

There is scope for some debate as to the timing of the sequence of events within the opening of the seals (Rev 6:1 to 8:5), the sounding of the seven trumpets (Rev 8:6 to 11:19) and the pouring out of the vials or bowls of wrath (15:5 to 16:21); it is a case on "wait and see". We are left with vivid pictures of a world on the brink of appalling disaster. Dan 12:1 describes the same period, focusing on Israel in particular: *"And at that time*

Christ's Second Coming

shall Michael stand up, the great prince which standeth for the children of thy people: and there shall be a time of trouble, such as never was since there was a nation even to that same time: and at that time thy people shall be delivered, every one that shall be found written in the book". Daniel was told *"none of the wicked shall understand; but the wise shall understand"* (12:10). Revelation certainly supplements what Daniel was told, and relates how judgments of increasing severity, and ever increasing frequency will be imposed. After all, it is to be God's Day of Vengeance, which the persecuted godly have been crying out for since the Psalms were written around three thousand years ago. The most alarmist environmentalists take into account only the physical impact of portentous signs; God takes into account the underlying moral causes.

We are not told to what extent, if any, God is going to allow mankind's mistreatment of the planet, such as global warming and pollution, to contribute to the coming judgment. Some of the disasters are suggestive of this, but others are clearly what insurers call "acts of God". Reading the descriptions of some of the trumpet and bowls of wrath judgments, one feels that the Creator of the universe is going to use astronomical and other means at His disposal to strike terror in the hearts of unrepentant mankind, as well as setting free hitherto imprisoned evil spiritual forces (Revelation chapter 9) to add to human misery through their last desperate activities before their ultimate fate. God is going to be blamed even by those who had previously called themselves atheists: (They) *"said to the mountains and rocks, Fall on us, and hide us from the face of him that sitteth on the throne, and from the wrath of the Lamb"* (Rev 6:16); (they) *"blasphemed the God of heaven because of their pains and their sores, and repented not of their deeds"* (Rev 16:11). Atheism will soon have had its day.

The trumpet judgments listed in Revelation chapter 8 are presented with a third of the intensity of the later bowls of wrath judgments of Revelation 16, but with precisely the famine impacting environmental effects one would expect from meteor, comet or asteroid strikes. Widespread famine is one of the inevitable causes of military invasions, genocide and land grabbing. It is all due to happen during the coming Great Tribulation. The culminating bowl of wrath judgment reflects something of the immense seismic, global convulsions which will be necessary to recondition this polluted old world for later Millennial blessing: *"There was a great earthquake, such as was not since men were upon the earth, so mighty an earthquake, and so great…..And every island fled away, and the mountains were not found"* (Rev 16:18, 20). We must remember that this wonderful final book of the Bible had to be presented in a way that earlier generations could at least partly understand. Other judgments reflect atmospheric catastrophe before environmental regeneration.

14. SATAN'S FINAL BID FOR GODHOOD

We now consider other aspects and sinister personalities of the Day of Vengeance of our God. I do not propose in this little book to attempt to preview all that is prophesied to happen between the Rapture and Coming in Power. But we should be aware of the ambitions of Satan, the Devil, for this short period, where he features prominently before his thousand year incarceration and final consignment to hell.

We are told that long ago, probably before the creation of the world, Lucifer, as he was then called, was the most powerful of all angelic beings – *"the covering cherub"*. Pride got the better of him. He aspired to be like God: *"How you are fallen from heaven, O Lucifer, son of the morning! How you are cut down to the ground, You who weakened the nations! For you have said in your heart: 'I will ascend into heaven, I will exalt my throne above the stars of God; I will also sit on the mount of the congregation on the farthest sides of the north; I will ascend above the heights of the clouds, I will be like the Most High.' Yet you shall be brought down to Sheol, to the lowest depths of the Pit"* (Isa 14:12-15 NKJV). Regarding his future, we read: *"And I saw an angel come down from heaven, having the key of the bottomless pit and a great chain in his hand. And he laid hold on the dragon, that old serpent, which is the Devil, and Satan, and bound him a thousand years"* (Rev 20:1-2). His latter imprisonment follows almost immediately Christ's Coming in Power. That final humiliation has yet to be accomplished; in the meantime Satan has limited rights of access to Heaven to accuse God's people.

Make no mistake, although God places severe restrictions upon him, and he has known since Calvary that ultimately he is doomed, Satan is still *"the prince of the power of the air, the spirit that now worketh in the children of disobedience"* (Eph 2:2); he is still *"your adversary the devil, as a roaring lion, (walking) about, seeking whom he may devour"* (I Pet 5:8); he is still *"the accuser of our brethren..... which accused them before our God day and night"* (Rev 12:10). But once the Church, the present ambassadors for Christ, constituting salt and light in this world, is called home at the Rapture, Satan will become increasingly active and desperate: *"Rejoice, ye heavens, and ye that dwell in them. Woe to the inhabiters of the earth and of the sea! for the devil is come down unto you, having great wrath, because he knoweth that he hath but a short time"* (Rev 12:12).

As we noted in the previous section, Satan has ready to launch into action his Antichrist or false Christ, also called the man of sin: *"Let no man deceive you by any means: for that day shall not come, except there come a falling away first, and that man of sin be revealed, the son of perdition; who opposeth and exalteth himself above all that is called God, or that is worshipped; so that he as God sitteth in the temple of God, shewing himself that he is God"* (II Thess 2:3-4).

We will see at Section 16 the evidence for a future seven year false covenant between the opening and climactic events of Christ's Second Coming. There must evidently be a brief interval between the Rapture and the start of those seven years, because

Satan does not know the timing of the Rapture any more than we do. We have already seen something of the last desperate attempts of Satan to survive and achieve his ancient ambitions to *"exalt* (his) *throne above the stars of God"; to "be like the Most High."* We observed at Section 10 that the world will be thrown into crisis by the disappearance of multitudes at the Rapture. Evidently Satan will seize this opportunity to provide a false stability to a panic-stricken world desperate for strong and decisive leadership. He will speedily go into action with his Antichrist or Beast and his master plan of delusion. This person is depicted as the first Horseman of the Apocalypse. But God goes into action too and pre-empts every attempt by Satan to set up a successful rival king, despite his initial conquests and very brief receipt of the fallen world's adulation and wonder; Christ is always in total control. *"And I saw when the Lamb opened one of the seals, and I heard, as it were the noise of thunder, one of the four beasts saying, Come and see. And I saw, and behold a white horse: and he that sat on him had a bow; and a crown was given unto him: and he went forth conquering, and to conquer"* (Rev 6:1-2). His bow is arrowless, and his crown or wreath is inferior to that of Christ at His later Return in Power. All that the following "Horsemen" can do is to bring war, death and disaster.

In Revelation chapter 13 we are told of two wild beasts or monsters - *therion* in Greek. The world will admire them, but wild beasts is God's description of them. The First Beast is directly subordinate to the Dragon - *"And the great dragon was cast out, that old serpent, called the Devil, and Satan, which deceiveth the whole world:"* (Rev 12:9). We are told: *"And they worshipped the dragon which gave power unto the beast: and they worshipped the beast, saying, Who is like unto the beast? who is able to make war with him? And there was given unto him a mouth speaking great things and blasphemies; and power was given unto him to continue forty and two months"* (13:4-5). Early in His ministry Jesus gave the grim warning to the recalcitrant religious leaders: *"I am come in my Father's name, and ye receive me not: if another shall come in his own name, him ye will receive"*

(Jn 5:43). The deception will be diabolically cunning. We will see the significance of the 42 months at Section 16.

The Second Beast is introduced in Rev 13:11-12: *"I beheld another beast coming up out of the earth; and he had two horns like a lamb, and he spake as a dragon. And he exerciseth all the power of the first beast before him, and causeth the earth and them which dwell therein to worship the first beast, whose deadly wound was healed"* (Rev 13:11-12). Apparently, although it a difficult passage to interpret and not all agree, there is to be some sort of blasphemous mimicry of Calvary with a false death and resurrection. Thereafter in Revelation the Second Beast is more often referred to as the False Prophet.

Almost everybody has heard of the dreaded "mark of the beast", identified mystically as 666 and described thus: *"And he causeth all, both small and great, rich and poor, free and bond, to receive a mark in their right hand, or in their foreheads: And that no man might buy or sell, save he that had the mark, or the name of the beast, or the number of his name"* (Rev 13:16-17). Not so long ago this prophecy was more difficult to comprehend, but, in these days of electronic tags and so forth, we can see how easily it could be done. I include this subject to remind people that it is incredibly dangerous to gamble with the salvation of one's soul to the point of being unsaved and therefore left behind at the Rapture. The pressures will be intolerable, although we are reassured that countless millions will be saved during the Tribulation Period. As for the others, we read: *"And the smoke of their torment ascendeth up for ever and ever: and they have no rest day nor night, who worship the beast and his image, and whosoever receiveth the mark of his name"* (Rev 14:11). Receiving the mark of the Beast amounts to acknowledging and worshipping Satan; there can be no salvation thereafter.

15. ISRAEL - THE SIDE-LINED CHOSEN PEOPLE

Just as two thousand years ago it was impossible to grasp fully the implications of Christ's First Coming without recognising the following three factors, so it is impossible to grasp the full implications of His Second Coming without recognising the same factors:-

   a. Christ's full Deity and humanity
   b. His dual Saviour and Kingly roles
   c. The interplay throughout the past, present and future between Israel and the Gentiles in God's plan of the ages.

The first of these three is not in dispute among those who believe the Bible to be the word of God. The second is generally accepted, although millions of those who pray *"Thy Kingdom come"* seem to be unaware that Jesus Christ is to reign unopposed for a thousand years following His Second Coming. The third, namely the contrasting roles of Jew and Gentile in God's plan of the ages, is for many a huge stumbling block, and is at the root of much of the current apathy and even scoffing among nominal and even believing Christians.

"God finished with the Jews when they crucified Jesus" has been a common misconception for nineteen centuries. The theory is that everybody else can be forgiven almost indefinitely, but that Jesus' plea, *"Father forgive them, for they know not what they do",* fell on deaf ears! It is an appalling indictment upon God and is utterly baseless. The great Reformers, while recapturing the first two of the above, failed to re-establish the third. We may reasonably assume that God, in order to permit what dispersed Israel was to endure during the following centuries, allowed this blind spot.

When we consider what are clearly unconditional, unfulfilled end-time prophecies, we frequently find detailed mentions of Israel – both the people and the geography. Now, as the signs of the times come ever more into focus, it is vital to get such matters in perspective before studying what is to happen on earth, especially between the Rapture and the climactic Coming in Power.

Jews are often referred to, sometimes cynically, as "the Chosen People". Nothing in the New Testament negates such verses as: *"O ye seed of Israel his servant, ye children of Jacob, his chosen ones"* (I Chron 16:13): *"The LORD has chosen Jacob for Himself, Israel for His special treasure"* (Ps 135:4); there are many similar statements. Actually the term "Jew" was not used until after the return of Judah from Babylonian captivity; however it has long been widely assumed to refer to all Israelites or Hebrews, so for convenience I shall use it that way. They were chosen by God in the person of Abraham, and in the following two generations narrowed down to the offspring of Isaac and then Jacob, to whom God gave the name Israel, hence the term "Children of Israel". This "chosen" title allowed no scope for pride, although, if we read the Gospel accounts, we find that pride was commonplace and still is among some Orthodox Jews. *"The LORD did not set his love upon you, nor choose you, because ye were more in number than any people; for ye were the fewest of all people"* (Deut 7:7).

Jews are the people through whom God brought His Son as Saviour into this world, therefore they have been immensely privileged; and He has yet more important plans for them. Jesus was a Jew, and as the Son of Man still is a Jew, the Son of David, a Messianic title. But, while He gave them certain unique privileges, He balanced these with unique responsibilities and severe penalties for failure. Isaiah's sad commentary shortly after the deportation by Nineveh of the Northern tribes was: *"But they rebelled, and vexed his holy Spirit: therefore he was turned to be their enemy, and he fought against them"* (Isa 63:10). Deuteronomy chapter 28, written shortly before the death of Moses three and a half thousand years ago, gives the most comprehensive list of blessings and penalties, with chapter 30 listing conditions for ultimate reinstatement. The nation's subsequent history has borne out perfectly all that God recorded there. *"For I am with thee, saith the LORD, to save thee: though I make a full end of all nations whither I have scattered thee, yet will I not make a full end of thee: but I will correct thee in measure, and will not leave thee altogether unpunished."* (Jer 30:11). Well into the Church age Paul asked: *"Hath God cast away his people? God forbid. For I also am an Israelite, of the seed of Abraham, of the tribe of Benjamin"* (Rom 11:1).

The common misconception that the Church has replaced Israel lies at the root of most Anti-Semitism within Christendom. It is a very grave error. It emasculates the significance of much of the Bible's end-time prophecy, which in turn discredits the relevance of Holy Scripture in the eyes of the world. Sadly, almost as many Protestants as Roman Catholics give an affirmative answer to Paul's rhetorical question, *"Hath God cast away his people?"* (Rom 11:1). No wonder so many are asleep to the signs of the times! For seventy years since the re-establishment of the Israeli nation, we have heard repeated, in defiance of God's assurances, the ancient cry *"let us cut them off from being a nation; that the name of Israel may be no more in remembrance"* (Ps 83:4)

However few things are clearer than that Jews have only themselves to blame for their long history of misfortunes and persecution: *"But though he had done so many miracles before them, yet they believed not on him"* (Jn 12:37). They persecuted the early Church even during the time of the Acts of the Apostles. So it was not surprising that, particularly after the Emperor Constantine declared his empire to be officially Christian, without any preaching of repentance and true conversion, Jews were ostracised and persecuted, at least by nominal Christians. The Crusaders, England under Edward I, Spain under the Inquisition, Russia during the Pogroms and Germany under Hitler were equally guilty.

Texts such as Gal 3:28-29 are often quoted to prove that God no longer recognises Jews: *"There is neither Jew nor Greek, there is neither bond nor free, there is neither male nor female: for ye are all one in Christ Jesus."* The context does tell us that we share the same means of salvation, but Jew and Gentile are no more discontinued on earth than male and female, slave and free! There is massive evidence from Acts to Revelation that God still recognises Jews and has special purposes for them; compare: *"Give none offence, neither to the Jews, nor to the Gentiles, nor to the church of God"* (I Cor 10:32) etc. The redeemed of both classes co-exist within the Church, where Gentiles have for nineteen centuries made up the vast majority.

In the meanwhile we Gentiles are the beneficiaries of their national unbelief: It took the Apostles a little time to accept the truth: *"Then Peter opened his mouth, and said, Of a truth I perceive that God is no respecter of persons: But in every nation he that feareth him, and worketh righteousness, is accepted with him"* (Acts 10:34-35).

The Old Testament repeatedly foretells the comings of a royal Christ who should reign on David's throne from Jerusalem over a regathered, regenerated Israel, and by means of Israel provide spiritual leadership for all the Gentile nations. If we try to allegorise these, we downgrade the reliability of the entire Bible in the eyes of the world. Some theologians take on a frightening responsibility.

16. WHOSO READETH, LET HIM UNDERSTAND

I have up till this point kept this book as uncomplicated as possible. In this section I am about to deal with something slightly more complex which Holy Scripture actually commands us to understand. I have already mentioned in Section 12 that there is to be an interval of at least seven years between the Rapture and Christ's Coming in Power, and promised to explain how we can be sure about this.

Two statements inserted by the Gospel writers are quite unique in Scripture; they read: *"Whoso readeth, let him understand"* (Matt 24:15) and *"Let the reader understand"* (Mk 13:14). The very timing of the words of our Lord to which these injunctions are appended can only add weight to their importance. We noted at Section 9 that Jesus was talking to a group of His closest disciples only two or three days before His betrayal. To class these as irrelevances or trivialities is a very serious matter indeed; and yet that is the treatment which they have received in innumerable churches. No wonder ignorance regarding Christ's Second Coming abounds. The context of the two passages is as follows: *"When ye therefore shall see the abomination of desolation, spoken of by Daniel the prophet, stand in the holy place, (whoso readeth, let him understand) then let them which be in Judaea flee into the mountains"*; Mark's account is similar. Obviously we cannot begin to understand without first referring to Daniel's prophecy and its context.

The key verse is Dan 9:27, to which we shall shortly turn. Jesus' reference to this prophecy of Daniel must have surprised the disciples, because it was popularly believed that it had been fulfilled in 187 BC by that exceptionally evil Greek Seleucid upstart king Antiochus IV Epiphanes, one of the most profane men in history who desecrated the Temple. But Jesus spoke of it as being yet future, demonstrating that prophecies may intentionally have secondary or even tertiary relevance, with the earlier fulfilment being less important than the final one. A further secondary fulfilment was when the Emperor Caligula, against the advice of Herod Agrippa I, tried to set up an image of himself in the temple a few years into the Church Age; he died in 41 AD before his orders could be carried out. That was not God's sanctioned timing. Nobody, not even well-intentioned Post-Millennialists, can bypass or improve upon God's unconditional prophecies. According to the church historian Eusebius, Christians in Judea in 70 and 135 AD saw their situation foreshadowed here. They were certainly not wrong in taking heed and fleeing to the desert in 135 AD during the further rebellion against Rome. But those modern theologians called Preterists should take careful note of the Matthew 24 and Mark 13 context, which is about the return of Israel from exile and to a world on the brink of extinction but for Divine intervention, not the start of the long *Diaspora*. One of the main points is that so many of God's prophecies are for practical purposes, rather than merely for information, sometimes even being for the direct protection and benefit of His own beleaguered people.

Daniel chapter 9, referred to by Jesus, helps us to understand better why the Rapture of the Church has to take place, why there is to be an interval of several years between the opening and climactic events of the Second Coming and why Israel is yet to be so central to God's plans. I have covered all this in considerable depth in other books, and can give only the main features here, inviting you to read Daniel chapter 9 in full.

In v 23 we read: *"I am Gabriel who stands in the presence of God"*, the one who later appeared to Zacharias and Mary with unique messages of critical importance (Lk 1:19,26). He told Daniel: *"I have come to tell you, for you are greatly beloved; therefore consider the matter, and **understand the vision**"* (NKJV). This, together with the later commands of the Gospel writers for readers to understand, is unique among the prophets. If the Holy Spirit has taken the trouble to have these put on record, it is surely incumbent upon us to pay careful attention.

What must have been shattering for Daniel was to be informed that, following the by then almost elapsed seventy years of Babylonian captivity, there would, starting at a specified date, be a further seven times seventy years of responsibility for Daniel's people, the Jews, and that those resultant 490 years would be broken by a period of indeterminate length (which we now know to be the Church Age) before the final "week of years" or "septennium". *"Everlasting righteousness"*, which Isaiah and other prophets had foretold and we call the Millennium, cannot be ushered in until the final seven years are complete. Now we begin to comprehend the importance allocated to these prophecies. From verses 24 and 25 we learn that 490 years were allocated to Jews and to Jerusalem. From the indicated start date until Jesus formerly presented Himself as Messiah was 483 years, leaving seven years in suspension. So, following the detached future final week of years comes the "bringing in of *everlasting righteousness*" as the result of the Second Coming.

From verses 26 and 27 we learn that between the 483rd and 484th of the 490 years allocated to the Jews, starting with the point when Messiah was "cut off", there was to be a long break. The remaining seven years commence with the future appearance on the world scene of a descendent or successor of the one who originally sacked Jerusalem (a Roman prince) making, a seven year covenant, and after three and half years breaking it and setting up in Jerusalem an idolatrous abomination. Thus these allocated seven years of Jewish responsibility in adversity dominate the coming Tribulation Period. We may speculate now about the apparent Roman identity of this coming ruler; Daniel chapters 2 and 7 tell us more of this latter day appearance of one of Roman imperial origins. When the time comes it will be clear enough to believers.

It was specifically verse 27 to which Jesus referred: *"And **he shall confirm the covenant with many** for one week* (group of seven years)*: and in the midst of the week he shall cause the sacrifice and the oblation to cease, and for the overspreading of abominations he shall make it desolate, even until the consummation, and that determined shall be poured upon the desolate"*. Note that the covenant is to be made with the "many" or majority of Jews, rather than the spiritually discerning "few" or minority. This is immensely important.

Jesus Himself puts His seal of approval and confirms the importance of Daniel's prophecy. Only the minority or faithful remnant will heed the warning and take action: *"When ye therefore shall see the abomination of desolation, spoken of by Daniel the prophet, stand in the holy place….. Then let them which be in Judaea flee into the mountains"* (Matt 24:15-16). Revelation chapter 12 relates how this will happen: *"And there appeared a great wonder in heaven; a woman clothed with the sun, and the moon under her feet, and upon her head a crown of twelve stars"* (Rev 12:1). The woman is not Mary, as some have supposed, but Israel who gave birth to the Messiah. A comparison with Genesis 37:9-10 makes this very clear. *"And the woman fled into the wilderness, where she hath a place prepared of God, that they should feed her there a thousand two hundred and threescore days"* (Rev 12:6). This is the three and a half year period (using the 360 day lunar calendar) following the breaking of the covenant.

Two Old Testament prophecies are primarily about this refuge, but surely also have an application to a heavenly sanctuary of the Church at the Rapture: *"Come, my people, enter thou into thy chambers, and shut thy doors about thee: hide thyself as it were for a little moment, until the indignation be overpast. For, behold, the LORD cometh out of his place to punish the inhabitants of the earth for their iniquity: the earth also shall disclose her blood, and shall no more cover her slain"* (Isa 26:20-21); *"Seek ye the LORD, all ye meek of the earth, which have wrought his judgment; seek righteousness, seek meekness: it may be ye shall be hid in the day of the LORD'S anger"* (Zeph 2:3).

Lest any should doubt the "statistics" involved, the two 3½ year periods are also found in Dan 7:25; 12:7, Rev 11:2, 3; 12:6; 12:14 and 13:5, with their duration described in various ways, namely *"three and a half years", "time and times and half a time", "42 months" and "1,260 days".* For instance, the two witnesses of Revelation 11 are to testify for 1,260 days (v 3), and the woman in Revelation 12 is to be given a wilderness refuge for 1,260 days (v 14).

As my old pastor, James Sidlow Baxter, pointed out, failure to understand or take into account Daniel's seventy weeks of years with its long Church Age gap, by no means renders the futurist interpretation of Revelation invalid, but it does handicap our comprehension a little. The Gospel writers' injunctions to understand were not inserted to be ignored!

17. ISRAEL – HOLOCAUST AND RESTORATION

Satan not only wants to be the centre of the Gentile world's attention, but also of Jewish attention. God has always been and always will be in complete control of Israel, whether punishing or pardoning, permitting attack or defending. Consider the following unconditional prophecies:-

- *"For I am with thee, saith the LORD, to save thee: though I make a full end of all nations whither I have scattered thee, yet will I not make a full end of thee: but I will correct thee in measure, and will not leave thee altogether unpunished"* (Jer 30:11).
- *"Behold, I will bring them from the north country, and gather them from the coasts of the earth….. a great company shall return thither….. Hear the word of the LORD, O ye nations, and declare it in the isles afar off, and say, He that scattered Israel will gather him, and keep him, as a shepherd doth his flock"* (Jer 31:8-10).
- *"Yet the number of the children of Israel shall be as the sand of the sea, which cannot be measured…..; and it shall come to pass, that in the place where it was said unto them, Ye are not my people, there it shall be said unto them, Ye are the sons of the living God. Then shall the children of Judah and the children of Israel be gathered together"* (Hos 1:10-11).
- *"Behold, I will make Jerusalem a cup of trembling unto all the people round about, when they shall be in the siege both against Judah and against Jerusalem. And in that day will I make Jerusalem a burdensome stone for all people: all that burden themselves with it shall be cut in pieces, though all the people of the earth be gathered together against it"* (Zech 12:2-3).
- *"And I will pour upon the house of David, and upon the inhabitants of Jerusalem, the spirit of grace and of supplications: and they shall look upon me whom they have pierced, and they shall mourn for him, as one mourneth for his only son, and shall be in bitterness for*

him, as one that is in bitterness for his firstborn" (Zech 12:10).

God addressed Israel through Isaiah: *"Your iniquities have separated between you and your God, and your sins have hid his face from you, that he will not hear"* (Isa 59:2). But He also said: *"Come now, and let us reason together, saith the LORD: though your sins be as scarlet, they shall be as white as snow; though they be red like crimson, they shall be as wool"…..*"And I will turn my hand upon thee, and purely purge away thy dross, and take away all thy tin* (refining impurities)*: and I will restore thy judges as at the first, and thy counsellors as at the beginning: afterward thou shalt be called, The city of righteousness, the faithful city"* (Isa 1:18, 25-26). That has never happened to date, has it? The future fulfilment is recorded in Zechariah 13, we have already seen something of the future apostate majority and believing minority: *"And it shall come to pass, that in all the land, saith the LORD, two parts therein shall be cut off and die; but the third shall be left therein. And I will bring the third part through the fire, and will refine them as silver is refined, and will try them as gold is tried: they shall call on my name, and I will hear them: I will say, It is my people: and they shall say, The LORD is my God"* (vv 8-9). *"For, lo, I will command, and I will sift the house of Israel among all nations, like as corn is sifted in a sieve, yet shall not the least grain fall upon the earth"* (Amos 9:9); Israel has yet to undergo her baptism of fire or final holocaust before her ultimate restoration. A longer and more vivid account is to be found at Ezek 22:17-22. Keep an eye out for ever increasing international isolation of God's ancient but still wayward people.

It is a sad anomaly that Shi'ite Muslims, such as the bulk of Iranians and Assad's Syrians, should take more seriously their prophetic writings in their Hadith than many Christians take in such unfulfilled, unconditional prophecies as are found in Ezekiel chapters 38 and 39. Their corrupted version of this prophecy, which pre-dates Islam by over a thousand years, makes Shi'ites in particular believe that they have a moral right to destroy

Part Two - Biblical Evidence And Brief Overview Of The End Times

Israel. Their failure hitherto to do so is surely God's testimony to their error, which naturally some of them find embarrassing or irritating. The Hadith or prophetic writings contain various other seriously corrupted scraps of Old Testament prophecy; they genuinely believe that they will conquer the world. The 9th Century AD Hadith corruption of Ezekiel chapters 38 and 39 is fascinating, because it has so many parallels to the Bible originals. In the Hadiths an 'amutual alliance' - armies from the north, including that of what they currently regard as a recently Christian nation (Russia), are to descend upon Israel at the time of the destruction of the Dajjal (Antichrist) by A'isa (Jesus), Son of Miriam (Mary); but thereafter the armies (as in the Bible) will turn upon each other. Allah, they say, will destroy the enemies in a single night.

I covered in some detail this latter day invasion prophecy of Ezekiel in my *"Israel, The Church and Islam"*. It is God Himself who confronts the leader of the invasion. *"Thus saith the Lord GOD; Behold, I am against thee, O Gog, the chief prince of Meshech and Tubal"* (38:3). *"Persia, Ethiopia, and Libya with them; all of them with shield and helmet....."* (38:6). It had to be no earlier than the 1948 re-establishment of the nation of Israel and has obviously yet to be fulfilled: *"In the latter years thou shalt come into the land that is brought back from the sword, and is gathered out of many people...."* (38:8). Regarding the fate of the invaders, God said: *"And I will call for a sword against him throughout all my mountains, saith the Lord GOD: every man's sword shall be against his brother"* (38:21). Could this be the mutual slaughter of Shia and Sunni, the best known divisions within Islam? Naturally we cannot be sure, but should keep our eyes on the Middle East.

God has side-lined Israel until a future day, when a variety of prophecies given over many years, but conditional only as to timing, will be fulfilled. Ten of these are introduced by the words "till" or "until". Earlier we quoted Zechariah's famous prophecy to Jerusalem: *"Behold, thy King cometh unto thee: he is just, and having salvation; lowly, and riding upon an ass, and upon a colt the foal of an ass"* (Zech 9:9). There is such drama and pathos and incomparable love in His subsequent declaration: *"O Jerusalem, Jerusalem, thou that killest the prophets, and stonest them which are sent unto thee, how often would I have gathered thy children together, even as a hen gathereth her chickens under her wings, and ye would not! Behold, your house is left unto you desolate. For I say unto you, Ye shall not see me henceforth, **till** ye shall say, Blessed is he that cometh in the name of the Lord"* (Matt 23:37-39). That condition, as we have seen, will be met, not at the Rapture, but at His later Coming in Power.

Since the end of the 483rd year of Daniel's prophecy, when Jesus was rejected by His City and nation, the Church has filled the vacuum left by the side-lined Jews. But the Church, as we have seen, is to be taken to Heaven just before the storm breaks. So witnessing Jews, genuine faithful, spiritual remnant Jews, are appropriately going to do what their ancestors failed to do nearly two thousand years ago. Where do we read about these?

John records: *"For the great day of his wrath is come; and who shall be able to stand?"* (Rev 6:17). But he then immediately tells us of 144,000 specifically identified as Jews by tribe: *"And I heard the number of them which were sealed: and there were sealed an hundred and forty and four thousand of all the tribes of the children of Israel"* (Rev 7:2-4). He who created DNA knows the ancestry of each of us. The 144,000 are sealed to protect them from the coming storm, for the task for which God was commissioning them. The timing is clear enough from the Revelation context. It is before judgment falls on the planet itself (*"hurt not the earth, neither the sea, nor the trees...."* etc).

Now we are not specifically told that these are evangelists, but they are evidently sealed for some purpose other than merely protection, and immediately after their tribes are listed, we read of the great international crowd who are identified as Great Tribulation saints, evidently saved after the Rapture, *"who come out of the great tribulation, and washed their robes and made them white in the blood of the Lamb."* Again God's timing is perfect. These 144,000 **could** be saved before the Rapture, but then they would be taken to Heaven and not be available for the Tribulation Period! They will be zealous for God, but blind to the identity of their Messiah until God's Holy Spirit comes upon them with power, as with Paul in his day (Acts 9:17-18, 20). Just as long ago Saul of Tarsus became the Apostle Paul in an instant, so, evidently very soon after the Rapture, God will seal His witnesses to preach the Gospel of the Kingdom throughout the whole world (Matt 24:14). In fact it is fair to say, skipping over the Church Age, that the 144,000 are the latter day successors of the twelve disciples whom Jesus sent out to preach: *"And ye shall be brought before governors and kings for my sake, for a testimony against them and the Gentiles. But when they deliver you up, take no thought how or what ye shall speak: for it shall be given you in that same hour what ye shall speak. For it is not ye that speak, but the Spirit of your Father which speaketh in you ..... And ye shall be hated of all men for my name's sake: but he that endureth to the end shall be saved. But when they persecute you in this city, flee ye into another: for verily I say unto you, Ye shall not have gone over the cities of Israel, till the Son of man be come"* (Matt 10:18-23).

The promised restoration of Israel about which the eleven apostles enquired (Acts 1:6 with Deut 30:4-6, Rom 11:25-27 etc), will not take place until the Millennium, which we consider next; in other words, following the culminating event of Christ's Second Coming.

18. THE YEAR OF THE LORD'S REDEEMED

We have seen that the Acceptable Year of the Lord, the Day of Vengeance of Our God and Year of the Lord's Redeemed are about the earth; the last of these three is for the mortal survivors of the Great Tribulation. Back at Section 11 we quoted: *"That He may send Jesus Christ, who was preached to you before, whom heaven must receive until the times of restoration of all things"*

(Acts 3:20-21). So our Lord's Return to earth from Heaven, which had long ago received Him, inaugurates this restoration. Restoration obviously refers to something previously damaged or ruined, rather than something for ever destroyed.

In Revelation 20 we see that the last stage of the **first** resurrection is to follow Christ's Coming in Power and that Satan is to be bound a thousand years, out of reach of those on earth in their mortal bodies. We can consider these mortals in this section and the resurrected believers in the following one. The thousand years or Millennium applies to earth. I have dedicated a much longer book, *"The Millennium – Restoration After Retribution"*, to this wonderful theme. In Section 5 I promised to return briefly to one of the main causes of scoffing within modern churches.

A very common phenomenon is Amillennialism, which implies the refusal to accept the simple straightforward sequence of events related in Revelation chapters 19 and 20, leaving it open to every kind of arbitrary interpretation and dilution of the stated facts, including the astonishing assumption that the present Church age is the Millennium, thus leaving no room in their programme for the fulfilment of a host of unconditional Old Testament prophecies – prophecies so clearly stated that they require no interpreting to be understood. Thus unwittingly they would make God a liar. By no means all Amillennialists are scoffers, but it is reasonable to say that, within today's churches, virtually all scoffers are Amillennialists. It is also true that almost all so-called Christian Anti-Semitism is found among Amillennialists, though of course most are not tarred with that brush.

Only Matthew's Gospel tells of the segregating of the redeemed from God-rejecters following the Great Tribulation; it is a straightforward prophecy and not a parable: *"When the Son of man shall come in his glory, and all the holy angels with him, then shall he sit upon the throne of his glory: And before him shall be gathered all nations: and he shall separate them one from another, as a shepherd divideth his sheep from the goats;*

and he shall set the sheep on his right hand, but the goats on the left" (25:31-33). Bear in mind that the earth's population following the Rapture of the entire Church and the catastrophic events of the subsequent Tribulation period will be hugely depleted. The gathering together of these survivors in a world with its transport infrastructure in total ruins is evidently to be an angelic responsibility. This is not the last judgment, whatever title some publishers have given it.

Jesus continued: *"Then shall the King say unto them on his right hand, Come, ye blessed of my Father, inherit the kingdom prepared for you from the foundation of the world….. Then shall he say also unto them on the left hand, Depart from me, ye cursed, into everlasting fire, prepared for the devil and his angels"* (25: 34; 41).

We must remember that all those who appear before this so-called Judgment of the Nations or Gentiles will have been presented with the Gospel of the Kingdom by God's Tribulation evangelists. People are to be segregated as to their reception of these persecuted preachers of the Gospel, described as *"these My brethren",* at a time when befriending or welcoming such will be a capital offence, and when the obtaining of food or visiting in prison for those without the Mark of the Beast will be incredibly hazardous, as we find in Revelation chapter 13 and 14. Whether *"these my brethren"* are limited to the 144,000 of Revelation 7 we cannot be absolutely sure. Accepting or rejecting their message will be tantamount to rejecting Jesus Christ Himself, so powerful will be the circumstantial evidence of their genuineness as His representatives. It is not, as some have suggested, a case of those who have shown compassion and charity being saved for their good works, however commendable these may be. We have already seen at Section 17 that Israel will have been dealt with just as scrupulously as the Gentile nations: *"upon every soul of man that doeth evil, of the Jew first, and also of the Gentile"* (Rom 2:9).

These are the final recorded events of Christ's Second Coming. During the Millennium His presence will be represented visibly on earth by what is called the Shekinah Glory. We read of the future reappearance of the Shekinah Glory, a pillar of smoke by day and fire by night which had been the symbol of His presence which had led the Children of Israel during their wilderness wanderings. Ezekiel records his prophetic vision: *"And the glory of the LORD came into the temple by way of the gate which faces toward the east. The Spirit lifted me up and brought me into the inner court; and behold, the glory of the LORD filled the temple"* (Ezek 43:4-5). This is why the world's centre of worship throughout the Millennium will be Jerusalem.

We noted in Section 14 that Satan is to be imprisoned during the Millennium, and will be unable to tempt (Rev 20:2-3). The global environment will have been restored to Edenic standards: *"The wilderness and the solitary place shall be glad for them; and the desert shall rejoice, and blossom as the rose"* (Isa 35:1) – there are so many supporting Scriptures in the prophetic books for all these assurances. Survivors of the Great Tribulation will be restored to health and fitness: *"Then the eyes of the blind shall be opened, and the ears of the deaf shall be unstopped. Then shall the lame man leap as an hart, and the tongue of the dumb sing"* (Isa 35:5-6). Jesus gave a foretaste of this at His First Coming. The potential human lifespan will be extended to a thousand years, and those previously likened to sheep will never die, having already been redeemed. They will receive their immortal bodies at the end of the Millennium. Sin will be the exception:

Children will be born: *"Thus saith the LORD of hosts; There shall yet old men and old women dwell in the streets of Jerusalem, and every man with his staff in his hand for very age. And the streets of the city shall be full of boys and girls playing in the streets thereof"* (Zech 8:4-5). During the thousand years, Christ's rule with a rod of iron will make rebellion impossible. *"And he shall judge among many people, and rebuke strong nations afar off; and they shall beat their swords into plowshares, and their spears into pruninghooks: nation shall not lift up a sword against nation, neither shall they learn war any more"* (Mic 4:3).

However temptations can still originate within the human heart. Individual sin will not be totally absent: *"There shall be no more thence an infant of days, nor an old man that hath not filled his days: for the child shall die an hundred years old; but the sinner being an hundred years old shall be accursed"* (Isa 65:20). This is why we read: *"And when the thousand years are expired, Satan shall be loosed out of his prison, And shall go out to deceive the nations which are in the four quarters of the earth….. And they went up on the breadth of the earth, and compassed the camp of the saints about, and the beloved city* (Jerusalem, the Millennial world capital)*: and fire came down from God out of heaven, and devoured them. And the devil that deceived them was cast into the lake of fire and brimstone, where the beast and the false prophet are, and shall be tormented day and night for ever and ever"* (Rev 20:7-10). For a thousand years people will have had no option but to conform to God's laws; but ultimately those born during the Millennium must be challenged and their allegiance tested. Many will fail that test and share the fate of the deceiving Satan. Here is proof that sin is not the result of an inadequate environment, but comes from within a person.

19. THE HOLY CITY, THE NEW JERUSALEM

Now we turn to those Heavenly based ones, who have been raptured without dying and those who have been resurrected never to die again. Paul rightly said: *"If in this life only we have hope in Christ, we are of all men most miserable";* but he then confirmed: *"But now is Christ risen from the dead, and become the firstfruits of them that slept"* (I Cor 15:19-20). His resurrection is our guarantee; and He is the Son of God who never breaks His promises. We saw that the *"dead in Christ"* of the Church Age will have been raised before the Tribulation period. All the other redeemed, be they Old Testament saints or Tribulation martyrs, have to be resurrected following Christ's Return in Power, thus completing what is referred to as the First Resurrection: *"But the rest of the dead lived not again until the thousand years were finished. This is the first resurrection"* (Rev 20:5).

A group of Sadducees, liberal theologians who believed little about the supernatural, asked Jesus a trick question about a woman who was supposed to have been married to seven brothers, each of whom had died in turn without her having any offspring; they wanted to know whose wife she would be in the resurrection. Jesus, to the delight of the more conservative Pharisees present, replied: *"Do ye not therefore err, because ye know not the scriptures, neither the power of God? For when they shall rise from the dead, they neither marry, nor are given in marriage; but are as the angels which are in heaven"* (Mk 12:24-25). Contrasting Adam's earthly body with our future resurrection or celestial bodies, we read: *"The first man is of the earth, earthy: the second man is the Lord from heaven. As is the earthy, such are they also that are earthy: and as is the heavenly, such are they also that are heavenly. And as we have borne the image of the earthy, we shall also bear the image of the heavenly. Now this I say, brethren, that flesh and blood cannot inherit the kingdom of God; neither doth corruption inherit incorruption"* (I Cor 15:47-50). And yet, following His resurrection, our Lord could and did appear and interact with His disciples.

During the Millennium the Apostles and various Old Testament heroes, citizens of the heavenly city, appointed by God for the purpose, will have prominent ruling or judging responsibilities for mortals on earth. For instance Jesus said unto the Twelve: *"Verily I say unto you, that ye which have followed me, in the regeneration when the Son of man shall sit in the throne of his glory, ye also shall sit upon twelve thrones, judging the twelve tribes of Israel"* (Matt 19:28). This refers to judging in the form of ruling, rather than determining eternal destinies. Other resurrected saints will have lesser governing roles; Revelation 5:10 puts this in the future – beyond the Tribulation. It is not a current earthly role of the Church.

Part Two - Biblical Evidence And Brief Overview Of The End Times

They and we are to inhabit the place which Jesus went to prepare, and whose first citizens will be the Church, the Bride of Christ: *"And I John saw the holy city, new Jerusalem, coming down from God out of heaven, prepared as a bride adorned for her husband"* (Rev 21:2). Reading on, we see that it is both the city and its inhabitants; yet it is indeed a place outside our present creation, with its citizens during the Millennium able to communicate with the earth below. It is to descend from God both during the Millennium and then after this world has passed away (Rev 21:2 & 10). The Lord Jesus Christ, still the Son of Man, as well as the Son of God, will ever be there: *"And there shall be no more curse: but the throne of God and of the Lamb shall be in it; and his servants shall serve him: And they shall see his face; and his name shall be in their foreheads. And there shall be no night there; and they need no candle, neither light of the sun; for the Lord God giveth them light: and they shall reign for ever and ever"* (Rev 22:3-5).

PART THREE

ARE WE READY FOR CHRIST'S RETURN?

20. THE AUTHORITY FOR OUR CONFIDENCE

The popular picture of Peter standing at the pearly gates granting or denying admission on the basis of whether our recorded good deeds outweigh our evil deeds has nothing to do with Biblical Christianity. The simple fact is, that Peter, the other apostles and Mary the mother of Jesus, all still await their resurrection; whatever traditions may say to the contrary. We go to Heaven only on the basis of all our sins having been forgiven.

Earlier we quoted our Lord's words at Luke 21:28: *"And when these things begin to come to pass, then look up, and lift up your heads; for your redemption draweth nigh."* Now the term "redemption" here refers primarily to the redemption of the body, which is finally to complete the redemption of the human trinity (spirit, soul and body - see I Thess 5:23 etc) of those who are already saved or redeemed. Paul says: *"In whom we have redemption through his blood, even the forgiveness of sins"* (Col 1:14). But those who have never truly trusted in the Lord Jesus Christ are also advised and encouraged to take note, as the signs of the times point ever closer to Christ's Second Coming.

In the meantime, it is important to appreciate that our eternal relationship with God is determined by our response to what Jesus Christ did at His First, not His Second, Coming. That First Coming ended at His Ascension, when He had completed all that He had come to do. The apostle Paul puts it this way: *"But when the fullness of the time was come, God sent forth his Son, made of a woman, made under the law, to redeem them*

Part Three - Are We Ready For Christ's Return?

that were under the law, that we might receive the adoption of sons" (Gal 4:4-5). He completed the task for which He came: *"I have glorified thee on the earth: I have finished the work which thou gavest me to do"* (Jn 17:4).

When He returned to Heaven He did not relinquish His humanity, or the following lovely assurance would be impossible: *"Seeing then that we have a great high priest, that is passed into the heavens, Jesus the Son of God, let us hold fast our profession. For we have not an high priest which cannot be touched with the feeling of our infirmities; but was in all points tempted like as we are, yet without sin"* (Heb 4:14-15).

2,000 years ago God intervened in mercy and judgment and paid the price of our redemption. Our salvation is free to us, but incredibly costly to God in Christ Jesus: *"He was wounded for our transgressions, he was bruised for our iniquities: the chastisement of our peace was upon him; and with his stripes we are healed. All we like sheep have gone astray; we have turned every one to his own way; and the LORD hath laid on him the iniquity of us all"* (Isa 53:5-6). As our substitute, **He** bore **our** judgment. It was a once for all transaction, which we should regularly remember, as at the Lord's Supper, but never attempt to re-enact, as in the Mass. His sacrifice for us eternally satisfies the requirements of the Divine law. *"Therefore being justified by faith, we have peace with God through our Lord Jesus Christ: By whom also we have access by faith into this grace wherein we stand, and rejoice in hope of the glory of God"* (Rom 5:1-2).

Claiming to be ready for the Rapture is not a form of boasting: *"For by grace are ye saved through faith; and that not of yourselves: it is the gift of God: Not of works, lest any man should boast"* (Eph 2:8-9). The Lord Jesus Christ paid the full price on Calvary's Cross. The righteousness which believers claim and which God recognises is not our own; it is Christ's, but imputed to us. This is the basis of our confidence. Back at Section 1 we referred to Acts 20:28: *"The Church of God, which he hath purchased with his own blood"* – in other words it is exclusively believers who will be raptured. Such expressions as the "Holy Catholic Church" and "Universal Church" are Fourth Century distortions, supposedly incorporating both believers and unbelievers.

The hymn writer was right who said:

> *The vilest offender who truly believes*
> *That moment from Jesus a pardon receives.*

On the other hand the respected pillar of the community who says *"I did it my way"*, will be met with the Saviour's words: *"I never knew you: depart from me"* (Matt 7:23). When God at immense cost paid the price of our sin, we can hardly expect Him to prefer our own alternative solutions.

How good or bad we have been is not the question; *"All that the Father giveth me shall come to me; and him that cometh to me I will in no wise cast out"* (Jn 6:37). For the believer, being ready for the Rapture means that we are equally ready for death – either way we are ready to meet our Lord! Since the very first generation of the Church Age believers have in effect been ready for the Rapture, the opening event of Christ's Second Coming. For almost a hundred generations death has intervened, though with the assurance that *"The dead in Christ shall rise first"*. As we saw back at Section 4, we are living in times of unprecedented pointers to our Saviour's very near return, and so may not have to experience death.

Participation in either the First Resurrection or the Rapture as appropriate must never be seen as a reward; all the glory belongs to the Lord Jesus Christ. Whether any believer is experiencing a spiritual "high" or "low" at the moment of death or Rapture will not influence our participation. As we saw at Section 10, there can be no partial Rapture, no ruptured Church. The blood-bought believer can say with Paul: *"I know whom I have believed, and am persuaded that **he is able** to keep that which I have committed* *unto him against that day"* (II Tim 1:12). Our confidence is solely in Jesus Christ.

21. OUR PERSONAL OPTIONS

Despite the approaching judgment of this world, God **wants** you to be saved; we need not approach Him apologetically, diffidently or timorously: *"The Lord is not slack concerning his promise, as some men count slackness; but is longsuffering to us-ward, not willing that any should perish, but that all should come to repentance"* (II Pet 3:9). But **there is no alternative on offer**: *"Jesus answered and said unto him, Verily, verily, I say unto thee, Except a man be born again, he cannot see the kingdom of God"* (Jn 3:3). The way could not be simpler: *"If thou shalt confess with thy mouth the Lord Jesus, and shalt believe in thine heart that God hath raised him from the dead, thou shalt be saved"* (Rom 10:9). The reason that God can and will save you is simple: *"God commendeth his love toward us, in that, while we were yet sinners, Christ died for us"* (Rom 5:8).

The one thing we dare not gamble with is consoling ourselves with the idea that, should we not be saved before the Rapture, we can be later. We simply dare not try to negotiate with God under our own conditions. Back at Section 13 we saw from II Thess 2:9-11 how God will ensure those who deliberately put off being saved will be deluded, effectively putting themselves beyond repentance.

Accepting the Lord Jesus Christ as our personal Saviour and sin bearer is the one decision of everlasting consequence which we make here and now. He has known from eternity the decision which you could make today! But He does not rob you of the initiative; the choice is still yours. Lk 21:36 is a greatly undervalued and half-understood warning of Jesus: *"Watch ye therefore, and pray always, that ye may be accounted worthy to escape all these things that shall come to pass, and to stand before the Son of man."* When is it desirable *"to stand before the Son of Man"*? There is only one judgment foretold in the Bible where we should actually *want* to stand; and that, as we saw at Section 12, is at the *Bema*, or Judgment Seat of Christ following the Rapture. Standing there implies being worthy, through having been washed in the blood of the Lamb. And that is something anybody can do now, assuming they have not done so already.

Very different indeed will be the true last judgment. That will be the most undesirable moment in human history to appear before Jesus Christ at His Great White Throne. We read: *"And I saw a great white throne, and him that sat on it, from whose face the earth and the heaven fled away; and there was found no place for them. And I saw the dead, small and great, stand before God; and the books were opened: and another book was opened, which is the book of life: and the dead were judged out of those things which were written in the books, according to their works"* (Rev 20:11-12). This follows the end of the earth. There are to be only two criteria – firstly whether their name appears in the book of life and secondly their recorded works or actions during this mortal life. In fact all whose names are written in the Lamb's Book of Life will have taken part in the First Resurrection or the Rapture, and will therefore not appear at the Great White Throne. But absence from that book will be considered evidence of one's rejection of God: *"They were judged every man according to their works. And death and hell were cast into the lake of fire. This is the second death. And whosoever was not found written in the book of life was cast into the lake of fire"* (Rev 20:13-15). However Jesus, whilst on earth, said on several occasions that Hell would be more tolerable for some than others. The not uncommon attitude "Well, I'm going to Hell anyway, I might as well be as wicked as I want", is incredibly foolish. Jesus did not enlarge upon degrees of punishment, but He made it clear that they were significant.

Having trusted in the Lord Jesus Christ as our Saviour, we ought not to sin: *"Likewise reckon ye also yourselves to be dead indeed unto sin, but alive unto God through Jesus Christ our Lord. Let not sin therefore reign in your mortal body, that ye should obey it in the lusts thereof"* (Rom 6:11-12). We can be reassured by the fact that even Paul admitted his weaknesses: *"For that which I do I allow not: for what I would, that do I not; but what I hate, that do I…… Now then it is no more I that do it, but sin that dwelleth in me"* (Rom 7:15,17). God knows that we are still subject to temptation in these mortal bodies, and has made allowance: *"My little children, these things write I unto you, that ye sin not. And if any man sin, we have an advocate with the Father, Jesus Christ the righteous*" (I Jn 2:1). True salvation is eternal and cannot be annulled: *"For I am persuaded, that neither death, nor life, nor angels, nor principalities, nor powers, nor things present, nor things to come, nor height, nor depth, nor any other creature, shall be able to separate us from the love of God, which is in Christ Jesus our Lord"* (Rom 8:38-39).

The writer to the Hebrews asks: *"How shall we escape, if we neglect so great salvation; which at the first began to be spoken by the Lord, and was confirmed unto us by them that heard him?"* (2:3). Are YOU ready for Christ's Second Coming?

BRIEF CHRONOLOGY OF MAIN EVENTS COVERED IN THIS BOOK

This table is provide to clarify the sequence of some key events.

Several earlier dates are very approximate – authorities are not all in agreement.

The single question mark indicates the unknown date of the Rapture, whilst the double one takes into account the brief unspecified period between the Rapture and the false covenant.

BC

2100	Abraham called by God as father of the race through whom all the families of the earth would be blessed.
1900	Race narrowed down to descendants of Abraham's grandson, Jacob, given by God the name Israel – hence "Children of Israel".
1500-1460	The Exodus of Children of Israel to the Promised Land.
938	Division of nation into two kingdoms, Judah plus Benjamin and many Levites in the Southern one and the remainder in the Northern one.
705	Deportation of Northern kingdom by Assyria for idolatry and unfaithfulness.
597-527	Captivity of Judah in Babylon. Daniel active in Babylon and later in Persian capital.
4	Jesus Christ born in Bethlehem.

Brief Chronology Of Main Events Covered In This Book

AD

28	Start of Jesus' ministry.
32	Jesus betrayal, crucifixion, resurrection and ascension.
32	Day of Pentecost, birth of Church and start of Church Age. Nation of Israel sidelined in God's purposes.
70	Sack of Jerusalem by Romans, start of dispersal or *diaspora*.
1948	Partial return and rebirth of nation of Israel in Promised Land, still in unbelief.
?	Future resurrection of dead in Christ and Rapture of living believers. Israel returns to mainline in God's purposes. Start of Tribulation Period.
? + ?	Man of Sin establishes covenant with unbelieving majority in Israel. Jerusalem Temple rebuilt.
?? + 3½	Satan cast to earth, Man of Sin breaks his covenant and sets up abomination in Temple, False Prophet imposes Mark of the Beast and demands worship of Beast, Great Tribulation commences. Wrath of God progressively poured out on earth.
?? + 7	Battle of Armageddon, Christ returns to earth in power and glory, destroying His enemies, Satan is incarcerated for 1,000 years, final stage of the first resurrection. Millennium is inaugurated in restored earth. The Holy City, New Jerusalem, descends to within sphere of the world below.
?? + 1,007	Final rebellion and end of the world. Unbelievers resurrected to face Christ at His Great White Throne. End of time. The Holy City, having been withdrawn, descends again in the eternal state.

Christ's Second Coming